Donkey Tales
Stories of Redemption

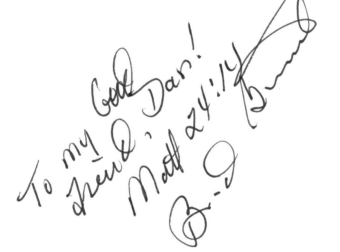

By Brad Bessent

Contents

Preface

I had no idea what we were fixing to cooperate with God to do. I honestly anticipated an annual mission trip, similar to short term trips I had taken before. Never did I imagine that God would lead Beulah Baptist Church in Hopkins, SC, with me as pastor, to plant a church in West Africa resulting in twenty-six mission trips in a span of six years. Only two of these trips were cancelled because of the military situation in the country. Because the collection of stories is extensive, I have chosen to break the journey into two parts. Volume one begins in 2007, with my first trip to Mali.

As the title implies, the donkey is a central character in my tale. One reason is the overwhelming presence of donkeys in West Africa as beasts of burden, and the other is the story of a donkey who talks in the Old Testament. There are those I have encountered over the last seven or eight years who were skeptical of God working through a local church in the way I describe. If indeed, God can use a donkey to communicate his message to a man named Baalam, He can use me—and you—to communicate His message to a world desperate to hear the gospel.

These experiences underscore principles of effective missional efforts of a local church. As I have heard our International Mission Board personnel say, "It is not the size of your congregation or budget, but of your heart, that matters."

Not too long ago I was visiting with a man who had been a member of the first church I pastored after seminary. As we were sharing lunch, I commented on how God seemed to be using my prodigal years as a testimony that anyone could be used to impact the lost nations of the world.

He said, "Brad, I think the greatest testimony of your life is to the grace of God that can restore and redeem a life for His glory."

It is with this hope—that someone who has struggled along the way may find recovery and restoration—that I intertwine some of my prodigal journey with this journey into West Africa. I pray this book will encourage others as it glorifies God. Any success in missions exemplified here is a testimony of God being willing and able to work through finite and flawed human beings.

I pray this book is enjoyable and entertaining, but I also pray that it challenges you to boldly answer His call—to rise up and say, "Here am I, Lord, send me." I pray the Holy Spirit will use it to actually change our lives so that every unreached and unengaged people group on our planet will be engaged with the gospel message. To that end, I pray we will be faithful, until all have heard and Jesus returns.

When Donkeys Talk
Chapter 1

"Then the Lord opened the mouth of the donkey and she said . . . (Numbers 22:28)

It was my first night in the African bush and I couldn't sleep. I was zipped up as tightly as possible in a nylon sleeping bag trying to avoid feeding the mosquitoes. As I have fallen into the habit of saying, I was sweating like a pig. The truth is, I have no idea whether pigs sweat or not, but it sounds like a good description of being radically hot to me.

Actually, it had been about three months since rainy season and the mosquitoes were not that bad, but I had saturated myself in 100% DEET anyway, and now I was zipped up in my cocoon, determined that malaria would have to search really hard to find me. The bug spray alone seemed to have raised my body temperature about 15 degrees. It was February, so it was only about 75 degrees Fahrenheit, but we were in a walled-in enclosure trying to sleep on the front porch of the mayor's guesthouse. The guesthouse is basically a cement slab, with walls made of mud bricks mixed with a little concrete and covered by a tin roof. It is divided into two rooms, and on the front there is a walled-in, covered porch. It was much too hot to sleep inside, but it seemed far too exposed to the wild to sleep out in the open like the missionary. After all, we were in the bush of Africa.

But it wasn't the concrete floor or the heat keeping me awake. I was still reeling from our incredible experiences that day in a remote village in Mali, West Africa. We had arrived in the city of Bamako the day before on a vision trip. The four of us—myself and three of our church members— planned to engage three different unreached people groups in search of where God might use our small church in advancing His Kingdom.

Steve, our missionary host, told us to grab our sleeping bags and whatever we needed to spend the night in the bush. That just sounded very safari-like to me, not to mention dangerous. We turned off the paved road and began traveling down a dirt road in West Africa, which permanently removed any interest I might ever have in four-wheeling.

As we rode along, Steve told us more about the place where we were going. "An African bushman discovered this village and came and told me that they needed the gospel. I was out here three weeks ago on what I think was the first time the gospel of Christ had been shared in this village."

Periodically he consulted his GPS to make sure he took the right turn in the road, as there were no signs. "I preached Ezekiel 33," he continued, "and spoke of being a watchman, and how we had come to announce to them God's good news. The villagers were interested, but there were no visible decisions. They invited us to come back and talk with them again. A couple of other missionaries in West Africa and I have covenanted together to be a little more direct in presenting the gospel to Muslims.[1] I was going to do a simple gospel presentation tonight, but you can do it if you like, and I will translate."

---

[1] The Malians practice what is called "Folk Islam". It is a mix of Islam and traditional African religion. If you were to ask them what religion they are, they would answer Muslim, but it is often more

"I would love the opportunity. "My mind began to race with excitement about preaching the gospel where it had never really been proclaimed before. *This must be what Paul and Barnabus felt like* as they left Antioch for the first time. *What must it be like to hear the incredible good news of Christ, when you have never even known there was a Jesus?* I began to consider how to preach this message clearly, when they have no background framework on which to hang the stories of Jesus. Steve suggested the "Romans Road," but since I'd never really learned that presentation, I settled on telling the story of creation and then heading to the cross as quickly as possible.

I began to cry out to God, Lord, please use me tonight. Help me make this clear. Help me get out of Your way so that You can accomplish what You desire in this village. You do not need me. You allow me to be a part of what You are doing. Thank You for this incredible moment of opportunity that You have provided for me. Only Your Holy Spirit can change a man or woman's heart. Glorify Your name.

We arrived in a small village adjacent to the one where we were planning to spend the night. Steve intended to greet the chief and essentially get permission for us to be in the villages. As the Land Cruiser came to a stop, children, women, and a few men immediately swarmed all around us. Steve pointed out the ground around a well near the car where African killer bees also swarmed. They won't bother you, he grinned, "if you don't show any fear." I hoped he was just messing with us.

---

cultural and true belief.

The children were covered with dust and their faces caked with mucous from trying to breathe in the dust-filled environment that was typical of that region most of the year. The scene could have come out of the first century. It is beyond difficult to describe the poverty in this part of the world, and yet, in spite of the conditions they live in, everyone wore the biggest smiles I have ever seen.

Our new missionary friend explained to the group of villagers that we had come to greet the chief, but we were told he was not there. Instead, some of the elders spoke with us.

"We are teachers of God's Word and we have come to share good news with the people in F-village."[2]

One of the elders replied, "If you are sharing good news from God's Word, then don't go there. Stay here and tell us."

"They are expecting us," Steve explained. "But we will stop by here tomorrow and tell you the good news."

The elder smiled a toothless grin, "That is good. We will gather the entire village to hear your story."

Having gained his blessing, we loaded back into the truck and headed for our destination. My first experience engaging West Africans. My first exposure to life in a bush-country village of Mali. *What beautiful and friendly people, and so eager to hear the message of God.*

When we arrived in F-village, we immediately began to walk through the village and greet people. The women were cooking what looked like French fries. Steve stopped to buy

---

[2]   To protect the believers from any future persecution we refer to their village by the first letter of what the name of the village sounds like.

some, and I thought, *Good—I can eat—and French fries, just like home, even without ketchup.*

"Here, try this," he said.

I spent the rest of the afternoon trying to wash the taste of those fried beans out of my mouth with lukewarm water.

As we greeted the Africans, Steve explained, in the language of their people group, that we would be telling stories from God's Word that night, and he invited them to come.

We returned to the courtyard of the mayor's guesthouse, where I bathed out of a bucket in a building used as a latrine—the place missionaries affectionately called a "squatty potty." After a hot day in a dusty climate and a long ride into the bush, the bucket bath was amazingly refreshing. Then we had our first African meal, eating out of a common bowl with our hands. It was something made of ground millet with some kind of peanut sauce. It wasn't particularly tasty, but these four newbie Americans were proud of ourselves for having eaten "African style."

After sunset, we made our way back into the heart of the village. There in an African courtyard by the light of a kerosene lantern, we shared the gospel. I don't know whether there were twenty people or several hundred. I could only see the front row of eyes, but I could hear the murmurs of many more. I was a little nervous stepping up to speak in this strange environment, but that quickly passed when I realized how near God seemed to be.

"I have come to share with you truth from the Word of the one true living God," I paused for Steve to translate. I began to share the Genesis account of creation up through Adam. I had heard of a presentation called "Creation to Christ." Although I had never learned that presentation, I knew the creation story and I quickly hurried to the cross. After sharing for about 30 minutes, I asked if anyone had questions.

"What do you mean, eternal life? What is that?"

After answering that as best I could, another one asked, "What do you mean, Son of God?"

Quickly I was becoming acquainted with the reality that these people had an entirely different framework of reality from the one that I was trying to introduce to them. Yet in spite of everything, the Holy Spirit was working, and I later realized God was never surprised by their questions.

After answering a few more questions, we invited anyone interested in knowing more about following Jesus to return to the mayor's guesthouse with us. That night, ten village men followed us back to where we were staying. The missionary and the African bushman who had first reported the village to him were both concerned the African men might not fully comprehend the seriousness of what they were being asked to do.

Steve said to me, "We want to make sure they count the cost and understand what it means to follow Christ. Because it is late, let me talk with them, and when I finish I will tell you what has been said."

So for about an hour and a half, the missionary talked with the ten men, and as nearly as I could tell did his best to talk them out of becoming believers. Obviously, that was not his intention, but in spite of his best efforts to dissuade them, nine men surrendered their hearts to Christ.

Then we spent another hour teaching them how to pray and more time after that finding out who could read so that we might give them Bibles. We stood around a wooden table in the courtyard between the mayor's guesthouse and office building with flashlights letting some read to us from the Bibles we had. The moon was bright and to me the temperature was very warm. The African men were wearing jackets and told us they were getting cold.

Finally, we prayed with them and said our good-byes. The men told us they were leaving before daylight to go to another village for market day.

As we prepared for bed, I had no idea whether I would ever see these men again this side of heaven. That's why I couldn't sleep. It had been much too incredibly exciting to see what God had done.

As I drifted between reflection on the day and prayer for these new believers, I heard the braying of donkeys in the background. A donkey can make some of the most horrible sounds I have ever heard, especially in the middle of the night.

As I listened to their braying, my mind drifted back to a statement one of my closest childhood friends had made to me. I was visiting him at the college he attended at some point during my own senior year of college. It was early morning in a dormitory shower, much like a man's locker room.

Out of left field, Terry said, "Brad, all I can say is this. If God can use a donkey in the Old Testament to speak, then I guess He can use you."

Terry was talking about the prophet Baalam who, at a time when he was not obeying God, found God speaking to him through the mouth of his donkey.

As I lay in my sleeping bag, I realized Terry was right. God can take a preacher from a small church in Hopkins, SC, and place him in an African village where he doesn't know the language, doesn't know much about the culture, let him share the story of Jesus, and by the Holy Spirit, let him see changed lives. Yep, I guess if God can speak through a donkey, I guess He can use even me.

God wouldn't let me forget this truth. On a later trip to Mali, our team had just settled in for the night. Usually during the first night or two in the village, the excitement of the day keeps everyone talking for a while like a youth group at summer camp. Finally, everyone was about to doze off in his or her mosquito tents (we were better prepared this time), when again a donkey brayed.

One of our male translators said, "Brrraaaad; your brudder is calling you."

We all laughed ourselves to sleep after that but once again I had a reminder—God can use anyone who is willing to make himself or herself available to Him. Sometimes, when God uses an old donkey like me, the seeds of a church can be planted in a village where the gospel has never been before. And sometimes those seeds will bear fruit resulting in other villages hearing the gospel.

Retrospect

While they may be called burro, donkey, or jackstock, I am told the correct name is "ass." The scientific name is *Equu sasinus,* and this animal is the smallest member of the horse family. Coincidentally, they originated in the African desert, which makes the donkey appropriate for illustrating the truths of this book. Donkeys are affectionate animals and need companionship or they will become depressed, as humans will.

The story of Baalam's stubbornness and God's rebuke delivered through such an unusual messenger is recorded in Numbers 22. God seems to specialize in choosing unlikely servants. This is the point as simple as I can state it. Sharing my experience is intended to say, "If God could use a 'donkey' like me, He can use you."

Consider that Jesus appeared first to Mary Magdalene on the morning after the Resurrection—not only a woman, but one scorned—and then you can move in any direction in the Bible. Abraham proved to be a liar and adulterer. Moses was a murderer hiding on the backside of a desert when God called him. Jacob was a con artist and Samson had a weakness for women. Rahab was a prostitute, Elijah battled depression, David was an adulterer and a murderer. Peter denied Jesus and failed at the most critical moment, and Paul was a man that heavily persecuted and tormented Christians before God called him. John Mark got homesick and deserted the cause, but came back later with a greater strength of purpose. We could go on, but the reality is God uses ordinary, fallible people, the most unlikely agents, to do His work in the world.

"Isn't it obvious that God deliberately chose men and women that the culture overlooks and exploits and abuses, chose these "nobodies" to expose the hollow pretensions of the "somebodies"? That makes it quite clear that none of you can get by with blowing your own horn before God. Everything that we have--right thinking and right living, a clean slate and a fresh start--comes from God by way of Jesus Christ. That's why we have the saying, "If you're going to blow a horn, blow a trumpet for God." (I Corinthians 1:27-31, MSG)

It's A Long Way Home
Chapter 2

"Not many days later, the younger son gathered all he had and took a journey into a far country"(Luke 15:13a)

One of the reasons I was so amazed that God would allow me to participate in a mission as incredible as the one we were experiencing in West Africa was the journey that brought me to this point in time. "Flashback" is what I think I remember my English Lit professor calling it. It is a scene interjected into the narrative that carries the reader back to an earlier point in time. At this point, I would like to turn the clock back three years prior to the events of chapter 1.

On February 5, 2004, I was working at my desk at the sign company my wife and I owned. About noon I got up, looked at my wife and said, "I am going home. God and I are going to have a long talk. If you get home and I am still shut in the study, please leave me alone."As I drove home that day, I thought, *Where do I start? How do I begin?* It had been thirteen years since my life had crashed and burned.

God saved me as a young teenager. My family attend-ed a Presbyterian Church, and I went to summer camp with our church youth. One evening, a missionary spoke and gave a public invitation for anyone that wanted to surrender their lives to Christ to come forward and have a seat on the front row. I sensed Someone pulling at my heart, and I walked down to sit with several others who responded to the missionary's appeal. After he dismissed the rest of the group from worship he led me in a prayer asking God to forgive my sins and asking the Lord Jesus to save me. After the camp, the Billy Graham Evangelistic Association mailed me Bible studies to help me grow as a young Christian.

While I am confident that I surrendered to Christ as my Savior that night as a young teen, I know that, like the younger son in Luke 15, I eventually wandered away from God to a far country.

"Sin will take you farther than you want to go, keep you longer than you want to be, and make you pay a price higher than you want to pay." Those words, planted in my mind by a forgotten preacher, were proven true in my own life. Like the prodigal, I walked into my Father's presence, demanded my inheritance, and traveled to a far and distant country.

Luke 15 tells us very little of the younger son's sinful behavior while he was wandering. It simply says, *"and there, he squandered his property in reckless living"*(Luke 15:13, ESV).

Too many testimonies of difficult lives seem to glorify sin by focusing on all the details. The elder brother had his own opinion of what this prodigal had done. He accused him before the father,*"this son of yours devoured your property with prostitutes."* Why did he make that assumption? Maybe that is how he would have behaved.

Jesus says in Matthew 7:3, *"Why do you see the speck that is in your brother's eye, but do not notice the log that is in your own eye?"*In my opinion, we rarely see the speck in another person's eye unless there is a "beam" or log sticking out of our own eye. After many years of ministry, I have noticed that many people are often critical of a certain flaw in others because they are wrestling with that same flaw in their own lives. Why is it that the same sin seems so much worse when someone else is guilty than it does when we behave the same way? God's Word warns us, *"Therefore, let anyone who thinks that he stands take heed lest he fall."*(I Corinthians 10:12).

The Bible also doesn't say much about the younger son's journey home—the time between coming to his senses in the pigpen and arriving at his father's house. We know that the prodigal was in a pigpen when he came to his senses. He picked himself up and returned to his father. How long was that journey? How far from home had he traveled? How long did it take him to get back? We aren't told.

For me, it was a thirteen-year roller coaster ride where I alternated between trying to draw near to God, and running away again. The first plunge was in 1991 when I returned from a three-week mission trip into Romania and the former Soviet Union. Back in the good ol' US of A, I could tell something wasn't right at home. After I pressed the issue, my wife responded, "I don't love you anymore. I love someone else."

It would be easy to blame my former wife for our marriage's failure and for my downward spiral over the next few years. It would also be easy to fall into the trap of satisfying the curiosity of those who share the elder brother's critical spirit and reveal the details of my prodigal season.

Instead I will simply say that the burnout of my ministry started a number of years earlier, and bad decisions on my part led me a long way from my heavenly Father. After my marriage finally collapsed, I was terminated as the pastor of the church I had served for twelve years.

It didn't take long to discover that a B.A. degree in history, and a Masters in Theology do not go very far in the business world. I began searching for any means I could find to provide for my three daughters. Sales was the primary option available to me, so for several months I sold water filters, home security systems, and cell phones, somehow managing to survive. While I did not realize it then, those days were much like the poem *Footprints in the Sand*. Although God seemed silent at the time, I now clearly see His amazing provision for my family.

Fast-forwarding a couple of years from 1991, God led someone from my past back into my life and blessed me with a wonderful wife and an expanded family. Mitzi had a daughter, I had three daughters, and soon we would have another one together. The task of providing for our five girls led us to become the proud owners of a sign franchise.

During much of this time, my relationship to God was only lip service. Honestly, I was mad at God. That seems ridiculous now, because I was the one that had wandered away, but it was my reality at the time. There were good times when I would draw close to God, but during those years, my life continued on the ups, downs, and unexpected turns of that roller coaster.

Getting off that coaster wasn't easy, but it began in 2002, when we received a Christmas gift from a couple in our church. These good friends gave my wife the book, *The Power of a Praying Wife*, and—you guessed it—they gave me the book, *The Power of a Praying Husband*.

I stuck my book on a shelf somewhere, but my wife began to read hers and pray for me. I have no doubt that her prayers brought me home. She never wagged her finger in my face and told me what a bad husband I was or that I needed to straighten up. She just cried out to God on my behalf.

Little did I realize that day in February that God was answering her prayers. As I drove toward my house, I could not help but wonder if my Father would take me back. *Had I journeyed too far from home to find my way back? Had I failed too often for God to forgive me and welcome me home?* It is really amazing what thoughts the devil will plant in your mind.

As I entered my house, I headed straight to the study where I got down on my knees and prayed something like this, "God, you and I have some things to get straightened out today."

God immediately whispered into my heart, "Not me."

At that moment, I vividly realized that God had not changed, nor had He gone anywhere. I was the problem. The whole problem.

The destructiveness of sin is beyond description. I had wandered so far that I was almost at a loss as to where to begin. I decided to fall back on a prayer outline I had learned many years earlier: the acrostic, A-C-T-S.

The "A" stands for Adoration, so I began reading and praying Psalm 145, a praise song. *"I will extol You, my God and King, and bless Your name forever and ever."*

At first, I was just saying the words—I didn't feel any-thing, but I prayed anyway. "God, I believe that the Bible is true, so I pray this psalm by faith."

I slowly worked my way down through the verses. "Every day I will bless Your name forever and ever. Great is the Lord, and greatly to be praised."

The more I prayed the verses, the more I began to sense this was as much my prayer as it was David's. I sang a few choruses, and I tried the best I could to declare the glory of God.

Then I moved to the "C" which stands for confession. I knew that God knew all I had ever done. I knew that confession meant developing an attitude where I said the same thing about my sins as God said.

So I took out a note pad and prayed, "Lord, I am going to list all of the sins You bring to my mind so that I can ask You to cleanse me of them."

I quickly filled the left column of the 81/2" x 11" page, and started down the middle. I filled it and turned the page over and continued.

Several times, I argued with God. When He said, "You are full of pride," I replied, *"Not me, Lord, what do I have to be proud of? I am not proud."*

Each time I disagreed with God, everything would just freeze—God would be silent.

And each time I finally agreed, "Yes, Lord, You are right, I am full of pride".

"Yes, Lord, I am a liar."

" Yes, Lord, my heart is exceedingly wicked."

With several pages filled up, front and back and two columns a page, I finally felt the Holy Spirit was through showing me the dirt. I was pretty disgusted with myself.

But the Lord brought to my mind the truth of I John 1:7, "the blood of Jesus Christ His Son, cleanses us of all unrighteousness."

It was time to accept God's forgiveness, so I engaged in a little symbolism of the moment. I took that list of sins out in the back yard. I put them in a pie tin, burned the sheets, and prayed,*"Thank you, Jesus, for taking my place on the cross. Thank you for carrying my sins as far away as the east is from the west."*

Then I took the ashes in the house and flushed them down the toilet.

I felt clean again for the first time in a long time.

I returned to the study, and continued to pray. The "T" is for thanksgiving, so I started another prayer list. I began to list all that God had done for me over the last thirteen years, thanking Him for providing a new wife, and for my wonderful children. I thanked Him for providing us with a home and food, and helping us support our girls through colleges and weddings.

First Thessalonians 5:18 commands us to give thanks in all circumstances, so I began to thank God even for the difficult days in my life. Most of all, I thanked God He had never left me, nor had He ever forsaken me. I thanked Him that He had been faithful to me, even though I had been faithless. I was filled with a deep sense of gratitude beyond anything I had previously experienced. I was amazed at how much God loved me in spite of my unworthiness.

The "S" is a big word, supplication—asking God to supply our needs—things that I usually just call "stuff".

I closed the three-and-one-half-hour conversation with these words: "Father, I don't know why you would want it, but I want to surrender my life completely to you. I will do anything you want me to do. I am tired of running. I am tired of resisting you. Please take over and be Sovereign Lord in my life. God, if you want me to make and sell signs for the rest of my life, help me do it to your glory. If you want me to sell this business and do something else, just tell me what. If you want me to go to Iraq and share the gospel in a public place and take a bullet, I will go. I surrender, all of me, to you, the best I know how."

It might sound a little overly dramatic, but it was heart-felt.

My wife told me later that God gave her a new husband that day, and, at the risk of embarrassing herself, she added that before that day, she had been married to an a—, well, another name for a donkey. Though I'm sure the animal is not what she had in mind, she was right. I thank God for the power of a praying wife.

God made a way for me, when there seemed to be no way. My prayer today is that God will do in my ministry what He promised the prophet Joel He would do for His people.

"I will restore to you the years that the swarming locust has eaten." (Joel 2:25, ESV). I hope to see God redeem the time that I wasted. I want to give myself to Him as completely as I can that He might use me in any way that He chooses. His way is so much better than our way. Life in my Father's house is so much more satisfying than life in the pigpen. But it was a long journey home.

Sin did take me farther than I had ever dreamed possible, kept me much longer than I intended to stay, and made me pay a price much greater than can be described. Never forget that Satan compounds interest at an incredible rate.

The wages of sin is death (Rom 6:23). When a Christian has broken fellowship with God, the fruit of the Spirit seems to wither and die. Peace is gone. Joy is gone. It all dies inside because God's Spirit has been grieved.

After February 5, 2004, joy did return to my life, along with peace. With the peace, I began to sense God saying, "I am not through with you yet," and much like Jonah, *"The Word of the Lord came to me a second time."* (Jonah 3:1)

In the days to come, a very good friend called my attention to Romans 11:29 and these words, *"For the gifts and the calling of God are irrevocable."*

As I explored what all of this meant, I began to talk with denominational leaders and with other pastors. I really thought I was just deluding myself—God would slam a door in my face. But it did not happen. I discovered that God's grace is way beyond amazing.

February the 5th, 2004 became a turning point for me as I realized I had come to the point of living in a pigpen, very much like the younger son, and I was determined to come home, humble and broken. God met me at the point of my brokenness in my study that day, in fact, He met me much like the father in Jesus' story, He ran to meet me, and He welcomed me home.

I believe that God the Father does that for anyone who truly turns to Him. The same precious blood of Jesus Christ that cleanses us from sin at the moment of our conversion will also clean us up at subsequent points in our lives when we fail God.

If you are like I was, let me encourage you to come home to your Father in heaven. Each day you wait is one day less you have to enjoy His presence. Why should we be willing to eat with pigs when we can feast at the table of our Father? Come home. God is waiting for you.

This is true for the wayward Christian, and it is true for the person who has never repented of their sin and come to Christ. God loves you and wants you to come to Him.

Retrospect

To this point I have shared my journey as it compares to the younger son, but before moving on, let's consider Luke 15 more carefully. Often I have heard preachers divide this into three different parables, the lost sheep, the lost coin, and the lost son. Maybe it is three, but I cannot help but notice that verse 3 says, *"So He told them this parable."* It does not say that he told them these parables. Personally I believe it is one parable with three parts.

It is the third part I want to ultimately focus our attention on, but let me suggest two observations before we look there. The first observation is related to whom Jesus told the parable.

The context is set in verse one. *"Now the tax collectors and sinners were all drawing near to hear Him* (Jesus)." Verse 2 says the Pharisees and scribes were all grumbling, and they were saying, *"This man receives sinners and eats with them."* It is this group, the Pharisees and scribes, the religious people of Jesus' day, to whom the parable is addressed.

It seems to me that as Jesus tells of a lost sheep, and the joy of the shepherd when he found it, you can almost see the Pharisees and scribes nodding their heads in agreement.

Jesus then tells of a woman losing a coin and turning her house upside down to find it. When the coin is recovered, her friends rejoice with her, and again you can imagine the Pharisees and scribes agreeing and understanding.

When He tells the third part of the parable and a lost son is restored, it is almost as if Jesus is saying, "If you rejoice over a sheep that was lost and now found, and a coin that was lost and now found, why can't you rejoice over a lost son that is found? Aren't people more important than coins or sheep?"

The elder brother in this story represents the Pharisees and the scribes by his attitude. The story concludes with an open-ended invitation to the elder brother to come in and enjoy the celebration with the father and the brother who has returned. What the elder brother actually did remains unknown.

For many years, I would say that I was much more like the elder brother. But somewhere along the way I became the prodigal. Looking back I am not quite sure exactly how it happened. Wandering is often very subtle, and that makes it extremely dangerous.

There probably aren't many Christians who wake up one morning and say, "I think that I will wander away from God." It is far more likely that we are guilty of what Hebrews 2:1 describes as "*drifting away.*"

Some years ago I heard an illustration of an elderly couple that bought a houseboat and moved into it on the river. One night, the moorings came loose, and the boat drifted down the river. When the man looked outside and noticed everything was unfamiliar, he rushed in and said to his wife, "Quick wake up, we have never been here before."

The warning in Hebrews 2 is that we *"pay much closer attention to what we have heard, lest we drift away from it. "*If we are not careful in our spiritual walk each and everyday, we will discover ourselves drifting and wake up one day thinking, *I have never been here before.*

Another dangerous thing about drifting is this truth: no one ever drifts closer to God. The direction of a "drift" is always away from righteousness and holy living.

That is what happened to me to a large degree. This should not be construed as dodging responsibility, because ultimately it all comes down to choices that we make. But it is a little choice here, just a small movement away, which leads to one more choice, and then one more, and so on.

James says, "Each person is tempted when he is lured and enticed by his own desire. Then desire when it has conceived gives birth to sin, and sin when it is fully grown brings forth death." (James 1:14-15).

We begin to grow careless, and that opens the door. Each step is a little easier. It may be as subtle as a decision not to pray one day, or a choice to be lazy about any of our spiritual disciplines.

The younger son in Luke 15 didn't want to wait for the inheritance that would one day be his. He wanted to enjoy life immediately.

Verse 12 says he walked into his father and said, *"Give me the share of property that is coming to me."* In a real sense, this is what we do when we yield to temptation. Usually sin gets to us through natural, God-given desires that we refuse to surrender to God, and try to fulfill in the wrong way. We demand our share right now, and we want to have it our way.

No matter what the temptations, when we surrender to them, the result is always the same. James said that sin, when it is fully-grown, brings death. Had the younger son not come to his senses in that pigpen and returned home, his unchecked sin would have eventually killed him.

The June 23rd devotion in Oswald Chambers's book, *My Utmost for His Highest,* says if we allow any sin to reign in our hearts it will kill the life of Christ in us. Sin left unchecked in our lives results in death to our spiritual focus. We will not see God at work in our hearts.

Perhaps our Lord intended the passage in Luke 15 as evangelistic in nature, as I often hear it preached. However, I cannot ignore its emphasis on restoration of a wayward follower of Christ. Notice the language in this third part of the parable speaks of the family. We are talking about a father and two brothers. God becomes our Father and we become His children when we surrender to Him at salvation. *"To all that did receive Him, who believed in His name, He gave the right to become children of God." (John 1:12).*

The younger son decided to return home and offer to live as a servant in his father's house. He realized this was a better alternative than life in the pigpen. We also can go home to our Father, with the same humility, offering ourselves to Him as a servant. Servants live better in our Father's house than freemen in any distant country.

While the son is still a great distance away, the father sees him. This son had done absolutely nothing to deserve forgiveness—he had done everything imaginable to offend the father. But this father was watching for his boy to come home, every day waiting. When he saw his son, he abandoned any fear of shame or disgrace and ran to embrace the boy.

We have never done anything to deserve forgiveness from our heavenly Father. We have done everything imaginable to deserve abandonment to our sins. Yet He longs for our return. He calls us to return. Like a shepherd with ninety-nine sheep safely in the fold, Jesus comes looking for us when we are the one still wandering lost. As the woman turning the house upside down for a missing coin, the Holy Spirit seeks us out when we are misplaced from Kingdom service. When we heed the Spirit's call and we begin the journey home, God meets us at the point of our repentance—our turning toward Him, and He helps us find the way back.

The father restored him fully as a son despite all that he had done. Our heavenly Father welcomes us back as His children, and His restoration is full and complete. God loves us because it is His nature to love and not because we have done anything to deserve being loved. He continues to love us no matter how unfaithful we may be. *God is love* (I John 4:8).

Aren't you grateful that our God is a God who gives second chances, and thirds, and even hundredth chances? God doesn't tell us that we will never stumble or fall, but He does call us to get back up. Maybe you have stumbled in your walk with Christ. Maybe you have journeyed to a far and distant country. Wherever you are, now is a good time to return to the Father.

How Many Wives Can I Have?
Chapter 3

"And the rib that Lord God had taken from the man he made into a woman and brought her to the man." (Genesis 2:22)

The air was filled with the pungent odor of shay nuts slowly cooking in the deep holes designed for that purpose. Even though it was February, the temperature had climbed into the upper nineties (Fahrenheit) and we were rejoicing and giving thanks for the large mango tree shading us from the sun's fury. Almost all of the men of the village, along with those women who had finished their morning chores, gathered to listen to us tell Bible stories. As is their custom, they had given us the best seats: homemade wooden chairs and stools, and a few steel-framed chairs restrung with vinyl cord many times.

We had returned the second day, as we promised. We greeted everyone, and began to share.

"We are teachers of God's Word, and we have come to share with you good news. I want to tell you a story that comes from the Word of God. There is one true God, Who is the Most High God. He created everything that exists and He created it out of nothing."

As we had shared in F-Village, we began with the story of creation through the point of God creating Eve for Adam. Once again, when we finished telling the story we opened the way for them to ask questions.

As we sat under the mango tree drinking tea, one of the men asked, "What does the Bible say about how many wives I can have?"

Steve grinned, looked at me, and asked, "Do you want to answer him, or would you like me to take this one?"

In a fleeting moment of wisdom I said, "Why don't you take this one," as I sighed with relief.

Like much of West Africa, this people group is polygamous. This is partially an issue of practicality. Farming is still done with antiquated methods and equipment, and in order to provide for his family a man needs many sons to work. More wives obviously increase this likelihood.

As I listened to Steve handling the question, I learned an important, yet simple, principle for future work in the villages: Allow God's Word to answer the question. Too often, we complicate matters with our own reasoning and personal points of view. We have a tendency to quickly answer questions for people in our American churches, which may encourage people to become dependent on us instead of allowing them to depend on God.

"In this story that Brad just told, when God created Adam, how many wives did He create for him?"

"He created one" several of the villagers responded in unison.

"Well, if God had wanted Adam to have more than one wife," Steve continued, "don't you think that He would have created more?"

Honestly, my first thought was, *What kind of an answer is that?* But I have come to realize it is a great one.

Rather than trying to appear to be the expert, Steve trusted the Holy Spirit to use God's Word to answer that question, and I believe he set the precedent for them to seek answers directly from God Himself in His Word.

One of the very first scriptures I had memorized as a young follower of Christ was Hebrews 4:12, "For the Word of God **is** quick, and powerful, and sharper than any two-edged sword, piercing even to the dividing asunder of soul and spirit, and of the joints and marrow, and **is** a discerner of the thoughts and intents of the heart" (KJV).[3]

Here is an interesting observation about a sword. We don't have to believe that it is sharp for someone to cut us with it. A sword is a sword regardless of our point of view. God's Word is a living Word, and the Holy Spirit who inspired men to record exactly what God wanted recorded works in the hearts of those who hear it to illuminate their understanding. It would be arrogant on our part to think that we can answer someone's question better than God can.

As Steve directed them to consider God's Word, I watched smiles break out on the faces of the men sitting around the circle, and their heads nodded in affirmation.

The chief even offered his own words of wisdom, "When there is more than one wife in the hut, there is no peace."

At the moment, I thought his comment was funny, but I discovered the truth of his words through later encounters with this people.

---

[3] I use bold with "is" to emphasize the current nature of God's Word. It is not an ancient religious document but a current Word from God to every age.

The man who asked the first question wasn't finished, "So if we want to follow Jesus, what do we do if we already have more than one wife?"

This is good, I thought to myself. I wonder how Steve will handle this one.

Again Steve looked at me and graciously offered, "How about this one, do you want to answer, or do you want me to continue?"

I was eager to hear the answer myself, as I had never been asked that question before. So I encouraged him to continue.

This time he got right to the point with his answer.

"God's Word teaches that you are responsible to take care of all your wives and children. Just don't take anymore wives."

Working in a polygamous context presents some challenges that are not typical of my experience in the American church. Several trips later, a woman accompanying us asked me, "How do I handle this? One of the women last night in our Bible study said, 'I am wife number two. Wife number one does not treat me very well. What does the Bible say about that?'"

Although I knew it was there, I had not really paid a lot of attention to how many Old Testament characters had more than one wife. Now in preparation for each trip, equipping our volunteers includes teaching them to answer such questions by telling relevant Bible stories.

"Are there any stories in the Bible that address the topic of how a first wife and a second wife get along?" In our training for a trip, I ask this of every team we equip.

The two incidents that immediately come to my mind, and often to those being trained, are the encounters of Sarai and Hagar (Genesis 16), and of Hannah and Penninah (I Samuel 1). We are discovering the powerful impact on our own church of trusting the Word of God as truth.

Steve reminded us early in our mission journey to trust the Bible. "God recorded it for all cultures. God's Word is reliable to answer any question."

Of course it is—we know that, but do we always trust It for answers? I am learning that the impact is much greater in people's lives if I answer their questions with the Bible itself, and not my own interpretation. This allows the Holy Spirit to take His living Word and use it in the depths of a person's heart to bring real life change.

One of the first scriptures I memorized as a young follower of Christ was Hebrews 4:12, "For the Word of God **is** quick, and powerful, and sharper than any two-edged sword, piercing even to the dividing asunder of soul and spirit, and of the joints and marrow, and **is** a discerner of the thoughts and intents of the heart" (KJV).

God's Word is a living Word, inspired by the Holy Spirit to speak into the hearts and minds of those who hear it. It would be arrogant on our part to think that we can answer someone's question better than God.

We Must Change Our Glasses

All of us look at the world through a particular "lens," or perspective, that reflects the sum total of our culture, our religious understanding, our experiences, and all of our life training. It's called worldview, and everyone has one. Every culture has a story, a narrative that shapes the point of view of every person in that culture. As an American, I have inherited a very Roman worldview of guilt and innocence. Many of the cultures of the world are very animistic and have a worldview of fear and power. The Islamic worldview is one of honor and shame. If we are going to be effective in any cross-cultural engagement, we have to learn to *take off our American glasses,* so to speak, and put on the glasses of the people group we are engaging. Sometimes we need a reminder that our worldview isn't the only one.

In an effort to help us prepare for these differences, the missionaries providing our first days of orientation taught us to ask this question:"Is the behavior you are seeing wrong—sinful, in other words—or is it just different?

Answering the question correctly requires that we set aside our own preferences and look to the Word of God for a specific command that deals with the subject. This reality brings us to a point of recognizing that God did not record the Scripture to be locked into one culture or one epoch of time. The Bible is an adequate source of truth for every culture and every generation of time.

Stepping into this village is like stepping back in time. The village we work in does not have electricity or running water. They cook over charcoal fires and draw water from a well. Because of these differences, I don't illustrate a story by saying, 'The other day I was driving down the interstate when I got hungry. So I took the exit ramp and stopped in at the drive through window and picked up a burger."

If there is a legitimate purpose in such an illustration, I have to learn how to contextualize the story or anecdote so that they can understand and relate to it. They typically travel on dirt roads. They don't have exit ramps and interstate highways. While they do have what we would call restaurants, they certainly don't have drive through windows, and unlike in our country, you cannot "have it your way."

We were walking through F-village on the second trip when one of our ladies, Terri, commented, "I feel like I just lived through a Bible story." We had gone to a courtyard to greet a family where a child had been born, and we were returning to our hut. An older man had hobbled up and requested prayer. We stopped and prayed for him, and were quickly reminded of Bible stories where that happened to Jesus and his disciples. I am convinced these African villagers often understand the Bible's stories much better than we do because their world is so similar to that of Jesus' time on earth.

Some of the differences in culture are more challenging than others. Sometimes the women in the villages where we work will want to protect their clothing. So when they are working in the fields, they may take off the top portion of their clothing. In trying to determine, "Is this sinful, or is it just different?" I discuss with our trainees what the Bible says about dress. It does tell us to dress modestly; however, the matter of modesty varies from culture to culture.

In the villages where we work, modesty for a woman means that she wears covering for her legs extending to her ankles. Her legs are not to be seen because that would be immodest. Out of respect for their beliefs regarding modesty, our policy for dress dictates that our volunteer women do not wear short skirts or shorts, or even pants for that matter—and they are not allowed to go topless either, in case you were wondering. But we don't ask the Africans in the village to adopt our standards of personal preference unless there is clear Bible instruction on the subject.

Wearing our "American glasses," we tend to think some of the African ways are strange or odd. Perhaps we should consider how they see our behavior.

One of the first cultural lessons learned in Africa is to never extend your left hand to someone as a greeting, or to offer them something from your left hand. This is insulting because the left hand is the "dirty hand," used to clean your nose, for example. We are so accustomed to handkerchiefs or paper tissues that we react to their behavior as odd.

Consider their point of view as shared with me by a West African. "I have noticed that Americans will blow their nose into a piece of cloth, and then stick the cloth into their pocket. Why do you keep your snot?"

Our own cultural anecdotes, illustrations, and even humor do not often translate into other cultures, as I learned in one embarrassing lesson on our second trip.

Steve had gone to greet people in a particular courtyard where a death had occurred. He left me with a circle of men and a translator.

"Ask them all the questions you can think of, and if you run out of questions to ask them, let them ask you questions," were his instructions as he walked off.

So I had asked as many questions as I could think of about life in the village. Then I told them to ask me questions.

"Can you have more than one wife in America?" one of the men asked.

"You are not supposed to," I answered.

"Is it against the law?"

I told him that it was, and I should have stopped, but I was nervous and I thought I would add some humor to the moment. I thought of how women in America sometimes have said, "I don't know why any man would want a second wife or girlfriend, when he has enough trouble with trying to make one happy." So I said something to that effect.

A significant discussion broke out among the Africans, and finally the translator said, 'They want to know why you cannot satisfy your wife."

Red-faced, I tried to explain my feeble attempt at humor. They laughed politely, but I am sure they had some serious doubts about me at that point.

Before we left B-village that day, they begged us to return. Steve had other plans and would not be able to come back. Another missionary, Marvin, was actually our host for this trip. I told the villagers that we already had commitments to be in other places, but that we would ask our host, Marvin, and if we could alter our schedule, we would indeed come. On the paved road about halfway back to Bamako, we had a cell phone signal and called.

"Marvin," I said enthusiastically, "God is out here and they want us to come back."

It was obvious that I caught him by surprise and he responded that we could talk about it when we got to town.

That night at supper Marvin said, "I don't want to miss God. I can take you back tomorrow."

We did go back the next day to B-village, and two wonderful things occurred. First, there were some men who became believers in B-village. Secondly, one of our church's prayers had been that our team would be an encouragement to the missionaries. When we left Bamako that morning, Marvin seemed to be somewhat tired and discouraged. By the end of the day, he had experienced renewed energy and great encouragement, a direct answer to prayer.

After our second day in F-village, we went on to engage the S people group who were farther north. We also spent a couple days engaging the B people group. Even though we did not partner to reach these two particular groups, there were incredible lessons from God on this particular trip.

In every village we encountered donkeys. One of our team members, Mason said, "There cannot be any donkeys left anywhere in the world. They are all in West Africa. "While that is an entertaining exaggeration, there really are an abundance of donkeys. I chose to view it as a humbling reminder that God was using me in spite of myself.

Retrospect

After the first trip to West Africa, I downloaded a ringtone for my cell phone that was a donkey braying. I know, crazy, right? But I didn't want to forget the lesson. The night that we were to catch a plane out of Bamako, we ate supper at Marvin's home where we also debriefed. I remember asking to use their Internet to send an email home.

Lanette, Marvin's wife, sensed some of the struggles of my heart as she turned on their computer.

"Are you OK?"

"How can I ever be OK again?" I asked her as tears began to well up in my eyes. "How can you see this—the lostness, the need—how can you see it and ever be OK again?"

With a smile on her face she said, "You'll be back. It's in your blood now.

We arrived home late on a Friday afternoon that February in 2007. After greeting my family and enjoying supper together, I headed for bed.

I bet I sleep all day tomorrow.

Wrong; I was wide-awake at about 5 am. I prayed and read the Bible and waited on my wife to wake up so we could talk.

When she did wake up, I went back into the bedroom to tell her everything that had happened on our trip. Oddly, when I opened my mouth, words wouldn't come and I just began to sob and weep.

She put her arms around me, and said, "It's going to be alright."

"No, Lord, don't ever let it be alright ever again. Break my heart for what breaks yours. Let me see with Your eyes, and love with Your love, and lead me to be Your hands, Your feet, Your voice in the world. Please, heavenly Daddy, never let me be the same again."

The busyness of daily life in the United States seems to dull my heart to the lostness of the world. It is so easy to become busy again working for God and allow activity to become a substitute for real mission. The downward pull of the flesh continues to draw us back to what seems urgent and what seems to demand our immediate attention.

Please Lord, help me never let the urgent replace that which matters the most to You.

They Shoot ~~Horses~~ Donkeys, Don't They?
Chapter 4

*"Brothers, if anyone is caught in any transgression,
you who are spiritual should restore him in a spirit of gentleness.
Keep watch on yourself, lest you too
be tempted." (Galatians 6:1)*

Way back in the dark ages when I was in college, I remember an occasion when I really wanted to take out a particular girl on a date. Finally, I got up the nerve and asked her to go out with me, and amazingly she agreed. As important as it seemed to me at that time, I don't remember her name. Oddly enough, I do remember the name of the movie, *They Shoot Horses, Don't They?* I cannot remember the plot, because I spent the entire night trying to get up the nerve to hold her hand. My car broke down on the way home and I had to call my Dad to pick us up and carry her home. For some odd reason she never went out with me again.

The name of the movie references the practice of putting down injured racehorses to put them out of their misery. After the experience of being dismissed from a church in 1991 and what felt like the abandonment of the entire network of friends that had been a significant part of my life, I thought I might one day write a book entitled, *They Shoot Preachers, Don't They?*

Somewhere along the way, I heard someone say that Christians are the only army that shoots its own wounded. That is not a true statement, however, from a number of perspectives. First, some churches, as well as other Christian ministries and individuals, practice redemptive compassion and engage in restoration ministries to various wounded people. Besides that, there are many groups other than Christians that are equally guilty of attacking their own.

Unfortunately, Christians do sometimes shoot their wounded, and sometimes Christians can actually be wounded or even destroyed by *friendly fire, a* military term to describe when someone has accidentally been killed by their own side. Stonewall Jackson, one of the South's greatest generals in the Civil War, died on the battlefield—shot by mistake by his own men.

Christians are already at war with the flesh, with the present world order, and with Satan and his demons. Our enemy is described as the *"accuser of our brothers"* in Revelation 12:10. We certainly don't need to do the enemies' dirty work for them by shooting one another. How often Christians are wounded by other Christians with idle talk and gossip? And how often does this lead to destruction of a life? Christians who couch their gossip as "prayer requests" are far too common in our churches today. We do well to heed the instruction of God's Word, *"No rotten talk should come from your mouth, but only what is good for the building up of someone in need, in order to give grace to those who hear* (Ephesians 4:29).

Jesus told us, "A new commandment I give to you, that you love one another: just as I have loved you, you also are to love one another. By this all people will know that you are my disciples, if you have love for one another." (John 13:34-35). Look at these two verses in reverse order. Jesus said that when others look at us, the way that they can tell we are followers of Jesus is by the love that we show toward one another. We aren't recognized as "Christian" by how loudly and proudly we sing, "Oh, how I love Jesus." nor by our eloquent speech, or our giftedness in any form of ministry and service. In fact, the Bible says, "Even if I speak in the tongues of men and of angels, but have not love, I am a noisy gong or a clanging cymbal. And if I have prophetic powers, and understand all mysteries and all knowledge, and if I have all faith, so as to remove mountains, but have not love, I am nothing."(I Corinthians 13:1-2). The distinguishing characteristic of a Christ-follower is that they love the family of God.

What really makes this passage in John even more powerful is how much Jesus says we are to love one another—in the same way He loved us. Jesus loved us so much that He was willing to stand in our place on the cross and become the sacrifice that would allow for us to be forgiven of our sins. In spite of our selfish rebellion toward God, and in spite of our stubborn pride, Jesus loved us enough to die the most painful form of death mankind has ever managed to devise. John 13 also tells me that I am to love other Christians enough to die for them, and they are to love me the same way.

Unfortunately we all too often irritate the soup out of each other. I am convinced that it would be much easier at times to follow Christ if it weren't for Christians. Sometimes I wonder about some folks that I see in church. It is like the longer that some people attend church the meaner they get. Have you attended a church business meeting, for heaven's sake? It sometimes seems like Christians schedule a monthly or quarterly gathering just to fight with one another. We would do well to heed the words of Jesus and die to self. In fact, most of us would do real well to get over ourselves.

I want to plead for the church to take a fresh look at the ministry of restoration. Paul wrote to the churches of Galatia, and he said, *"Brothers, if anyone is caught in any transgression, you who are spiritual should restore him in a spirit of gentleness. Keep watch on yourself, lest you too be tempted."* (Gal. 6:1). This verse starts out with something stronger than this English translation has suggested. The grammatical force of Paul's words is *"**even** if someone is caught."* The circumstance addressed by the apostle is one in which a person is caught red-handed in sin. There is no doubt about guilt. *"Even if"* a person is absolutely guilty of sin, those who are walking under God's control are to seek to restore that person. This word *"restore"* is a translation of a word sometimes used to describe a doctor setting a bone so that it can heal. Paul's challenge is that when a Christian brother and sister stumble in sin, don't take them out back and shoot them, instead be God's instrument of grace to set them back on the path of walking with Him. That definitely includes a rebuke, and sometimes may even require discipline, but the objective is always restoration to a right relationship to Christ and to the family of God.

During my own prodigal years, I wish a brother in Christ had demonstrated that they loved me enough to provide correction in my life. There is no desire to pass the buck or responsibility anywhere else, and I don't have any bad feelings toward any former friends. My network of friends had all been either tied to the church I served or they were fellow ministers. I got off course because of my own bad choices.

I learned the hard way that God does indeed allow us make our own choices. While we can make choices, we cannot determine the outcome of those choices. Every choice has a consequence. If I stick my hand in a fire, it will burn. If I jump off a tall building, I will not float upwards—gravity is going to pull me down. No one caused me to make bad choices. No one else set my life on the wrong path. All I am suggesting is I might not have wandered quite as far, had someone who loved me had been wise and bold enough to come alongside and encourage me to make the right choices from there forward.

Remembering the story that we so often call he *Prodigal Son,* would things have gone differently if the elder brother had stepped into the picture on the front end of the story? In the eastern culture, the setting of this story, an elder brother does have certain responsibilities for his siblings. As I see it, because this parable was addressed to the Pharisees, and because the elder brother was the character that represented them, the elder brother is actually the focus of this part of the story.

Suppose he had stepped into the scene right after the younger son had demanded the Father give him his share of the inheritance. Imagine the older brother saying, "Hey, bro, you are out of line. This is your Father you are talking to. Have you lost your mind? You need to apologize to Dad right now. If you don't get this straight pretty quick, I am going to teach you a thing or two out back. Comprehende, amigo?"

Recently we were discussing a discipline matter that had come up with the church in F-village. One of the believers was behaving in a way that was dishonoring God and destroying the testimony of the church. We acted decisively and exactly by the scripture. It turned out very well. The brother was restored and the church was made stronger.

One of the deacons in our church said, "Pastor, you hold the church in West Africa to a higher standard than you hold the church here."

I thought about that for a few moments and then responded, "You are right, I do."

"Why is that?" he asked.

Once again I thought about it and then replied, *"Because I can."*

It seems to me that many of the churches in America have drifted so far from the Biblical norm that the practice of discipline and restoration is a forgotten responsibility.

In Ephesians 5:18 we are told to be filled with the Spirit of God. In the verses that follow we have a description of some of the activities that accompany being Spirit-filled. We quickly agree that we will give thanks and that we will be joyful. But we often overlook the fact that Paul also says *"submitting ourselves to one another out of reverence for Christ."* (Ephesians 5:21). That is not something we can force on others. It is a voluntary submission to others so that we all might be encouraged, by each other, to walk faithfully with Christ.

Jesus Came and Got Me

Several years ago a good friend was on the phone on a Saturday evening. We were talking about the grace of God that would give a man second, third, even hundredth chances after failing so miserably.

"Are you familiar with the Lord of the Rings trilogy?" he asked.

"I am aware of them, but not familiar with them. Honestly, I haven't watched them or read the book," I responded.[4]

My friend explained, "Well, in one of the series, there is the good wizard named Gandalf. He dies and ends up in some dark underworld. He has some battles with some demonic type creatures and wins those battles and then comes back to life. I think about you that way. You descended into the lower regions of life, but you won the battle and have come back."

"That is an interesting description," I said. "Let me think about that for a while. Hey, my wife is calling me to supper so let me go."

After I had eaten, I went into my bedroom and sat in the corner where I normally go to pray or to have my devotions. *Is He right, Lord? Is that an accurate description of what happened to me?*

A very different but completely distinct impression came to me. It was as if God said, "No Brad, that is not *exactly* what happened. You took the wrong road. You made some bad

---

[4] I have not read the books, so I have no idea how accurate my friend's description of events is or is not, and it is not particularly important. I am simply relaying the conversation as it occurred.

decisions. You ended up in the dark regions of life because of sin, but you didn't win the battle. You were mortally wounded and down for the count. But I came and got you. I brought you out and brought you back."

"Wow, God," I said. "You are amazing. I don't know why You love me so incredibly much, but I am so grateful that You do. Thank You, thank You, thank You."

The truth is that sometimes other people will disappoint us. Sometimes we may find ourselves in a place where we are all alone. The reality is that God never gives up on us. The Word of God speaks so powerfully in Lamentations 3:32-33. *"The steadfast love of the Lord never ceases; His mercies never come to an end; they are new every morning; great is Your faithfulness."*

In Romans 8:38-39, the apostle Paul emphatically declares, "For I am sure that neither death nor life, nor angels nor rulers, nor things present nor things to come, nor power, nor height nor depth, nor anything else in all creation, will be able to separate us from the love of God in Christ Jesus our Lord."

We cannot ignore the fact that it is our responsibility to love one another in the Body of Christ enough to practice the ministry of restoration. God's Word declares in Galatians 6:1, *"Brothers, if anyone is caught in any transgression, you who are spiritual should restore him in a spirit of gentleness. Keep watch on yourself, lest you too be tempted."*

We have a God-given mandate to not shoot our wounded soldiers, but to nurture them back to a faithful walk with God.

Sometimes love calls for discipline. Sometimes love demands a rebuke. Other times, however, love calls for the exercise of compassion. Sometimes it is as simple as reaching out our hand to give someone a boost back on their feet. The Bible is full of the stories of men and women who were failures but were restored and then used mightily by God.

The word *"prodigal"* essentially means wastefully extravagant. The younger son acted as a prodigal, but his life was not ultimately wasted because he returned to the father. Was the elder brother the real prodigal in the story? I guess the answer to that question rests in whether or not he made the decision to stay outside the circle of the father's celebration or he decided to go in to the party.

Recently a man sat in my office while I shared the Good News of salvation with him. When I asked him about making a decision for Christ he said, *"I am afraid that I will leave here and mess up."*

I said, "I can take that fear away from you, brother. You will mess up. But God will pick you back up to go again."

In case you forgot, Christians do sin. We mess up all the time. Sometimes it is worse than others. The issue is not will we ever mess up and fall. The real issue is, *Will we allow God to pick us back up and put us back in the race?*

Retrospect

Do you remember the donkey ringtone? One day shortly after I set the ringtone to "donkey braying", I was eating lunch in a sandwich shop near our church and I received a call.

I had forgotten to turn the ringtone down, so most of those in the shop heard the ring.

As she was leaving, one lady leaned over and said, "That is the most obnoxious ringtone I think that I have ever heard."

Later when I had a moment to reflect on her comment, God seemed to whisper to my heart and said, "When my people share my Word without love, that is how they sound to me." God's Word says *"If I speak in the tongues of men and of angels, but have not love, I am a noisy gong or a clanging cymbal."* (I Corinthians 13:1) No matter how eloquent we are, no matter how gifted at putting together words, without love it is just noise.

Jesus said the single most important commandment for us to obey is to love God with all of our heart, soul, mind, and strength. He also said, however, there is a second commandment that cannot be separated from the first: We are to love others as we love ourselves (Mark 12:28-31).

Near the end of his life, as the apostle John remembered those words of Jesus he said, *"Anyone who does not love does not know God, because God is love"* (I John 4:8).

As we strive to be conservative and ever so orthodox in our theology, let us be careful to not forget to be very liberal in our loving one another. *"Little children, let us not love in word or talk but in deed and in truth"* (I John 3:18).

Bigger than a Donkey
Chapter 5

"Go therefore and make disciples."
(Matthew 28:19a)

Six weeks after our first trip into the bush country
of West Africa, I was back in F-village with missionary Steve;
Mason, a veteran of our vision trip; and two newbies: our youth
pastor, Ken; and Terri, one of the ladies of our church. I had only
thought it was hot in February—April's temperatures soared
past 110 degrees Fahrenheit in the daytime and remained in
the mid to upper 80's at night.

Since our last trip, a female missionary had brought
an African pastor from the city to conduct the first baptism in
F-village. Several men from a nearby village were there, and
witnessed the baptism. The gospel had already been presented in their village, so God had been preparing their hearts.
They said, "We heard that you have good news from the Word
of God." These four men from D-village decided to follow Jesus
and were also baptized that day.

We wanted to walk to D-village the next day to encourage these newly baptized men. The village was about
five miles away and we would need to leave early to avoid the
hottest time of the day.

As we walked back to the mayor's guesthouse, there
was a huge discussion between three of the African believers
and the missionary. Finally, I asked, "What is the conversation
all about?"

Steve replied, "Don't take this the wrong way, but they are concerned you cannot make the walk."

"What about Mason?" I quickly asked, "Are they worried about him?"

"No," he replied, "they think he will do fine."

Mason was over 70 years of age, at least 15 or 16 years my elder. I couldn't understand why they were concerned about me and not him.

With my freshly wounded pride hidden as best I could manage, I said, "Well, what are my options?"

"What do you mean?" asked Steve.

"I don't know, maybe I could ride in a donkey cart—that looks kind of fun."

He turned back to the Africans and shared with them what I had said, and one of them said something in reply. Before I could ask for translation, my three new friends were rolling around in the dirt laughing their heads off. Actually their heads never came off, but they *were* rolling around in the dirt, as they enjoyed the humor in what one of them had said.

"Ok, my friend," I said to the missionary. "Tell me what is so stinkin' funny?"

He was chuckling, but it was clear Steve was trying to suppress his laughter. "They said you are bigger than a donkey."

Thick skin being a requirement for missions—and ministry of any kind, for that matter—I joined in the laughter, at my expense.

So why were we going to walk? We had a perfectly good truck sitting in front of our mud hut. One of the first principles of missions I learned was the importance of a reproducible strategy of evangelism. The people group we work with numbers approximately four million, and less than .001% are Christians. If the gospel is going to reach every village, the African believers must reproduce and plant churches themselves. If we drove to D-village, we were afraid the African believers would use their lack of a vehicle as an excuse not to walk to adjacent villages to share Christ when we are not there. We wanted to model the behavior we hoped they would reproduce after we left.

For the record, I made the trip just fine. I may indeed be bigger than some donkeys, but I serve a God who is not only bigger than a donkey, He is so big that all of the universe cannot contain Him.

We had accepted a challenge of the International Mission Board to get involved, and they gave us several people groups to pray about, and shared the priorities from their perspective. We journeyed to Mali back in February on a vision trip to engage these people, and see what God had in mind, which turned out to be quite different from what we had imagined.

We journeyed to Mali thinking that we knew what God wanted. One people group had no career missionary assigned. But they did have one church in the U.S. working to reach them, a church only 30 miles from us. Their pastor had also previously served at our church. Too many interesting issues had arisen, we thought, for it to be just coincidence. Surely God was leading us to that people group.

But on the last night of our vision trip we—the four men from our church, Marvin, Terry, Mason and myself—had prayed and talked about what God was doing. Each one of us was certain that God was leading us to partner with Steve, who was assigned to the Bambara. Of the three choices given us by the IMB, the Bambara were the lowest priority. Even so, we felt confident God was going to take these 4 million West Africans and use them in an incredible way to reach others in their country.

When Steve had carried us to F-village, he had told us that on his first trip out there he had carried a mega-church team with him. Steve had asked them to adopt that village and work with him. They had said it was much too big of a challenge for them to undertake. As we talked that night, I couldn't help thinking, *if it is too big of a challenge for a church of 10,000, how can our church with an attendance of about 150 ever make a difference?*

God quickly reminded me of Gideon, another unlikely servant. Gideon was threshing wheat inside a winepress, hiding from the Midianites when the angel of the Lord came to him. The angel told him to go and deliver the Israelites from their enemy.

Gideon was dumbfounded, "Please, Lord, how can I save Israel? Behold, my clan is the weakest in Manasseh, and I am the least in my father's house." (Judges 6:15, ESV).

"I will be with you," the Lord promised.

Gideon mustered an army of 32,000 men to fight the Midianites, and set up camp south of their enemy—an army that outnumbered them tremendously and who were far better equipped to fight.

Then the Lord did an amazing thing in Judges 7:2. He tells Gideon that he has too many men. God told Gideon to tell anyone who was afraid to go home. "Then 22,000 of the people returned, and 10,000 remained."

"They are still too many", the Lord said. He tells Gideon to take them down to the water and tell them to drink. Then the Lord says, "Everyone who laps the water with his tongue, as a dog laps, you shall set by himself." (7:5, ESV)

With an army that is now 300 strong, the Lord tells Gideon they will go into battle. God did not want Israel to think they had defeated Midian by their own might.

God spoke very clearly into my heart that night in the mission guesthouse in Bamako, Mali: *You can be too big for God to use, but you can never be too small.*

I was full of enthusiasm as I picked up the phone to call the missionary and tell him the news. I was certain he would jump up and down for joy and tell me how wonderful this news really was.

Instead, when I said to him, "We want to be your partners and we will adopt F-village," without a moment's hesitation he said, "I will need you to come every six weeks."

After I picked the telephone up from the floor, I began to offer my excuses. "I was thinking once or twice a year. Our church budget is only about $300,000. We are a small rural blue-collar church. We could never manage to come that often."

The missionary said, "In order to make a difference, you will have to come every six weeks."

"Let me get home and share what has happened, and see how the church responds," I managed to mumble.

All of the missionaries I had met on the vision trip were fixing to leave the country. Some were going on stateside assignment for a year. Some were going on vacation. Some had meetings to attend. As I lay down on the bed that night, I counted at least 14 new believers in two villages we had been in a week and a half earlier.

The last words of the missionary had been, "I don't think anyone from here can get back to that village for about 3 months."

I began to weep and to pray. "Father, Your Word says, 'being confident of this very thing, that He who began a good work in you will perform it until...'[5] The missionaries can't get back. I don't know what we will be able to do. Please honor Your Word and keep these new believers."

We were back in F-village six weeks later and I had just been told I was bigger than a donkey. Little did I know how significantly we would become involved in engaging this village with the gospel. The task was so much bigger than our church. Maybe I am bigger than some of the donkeys, but this task is overwhelmingly bigger than our church. I was fixing to learn that God was bigger than I had ever conceived. As I write these words, Beulah has made 26 trips into this village over the space of 6 years. We spent more than half a million dollars to fund these trips, and not one penny came out of the church budget.

The financial issue was not the only cost required of our team members. God accepted many different kinds of sacrifices from His people in our church, and blessed us all in

---

[5] My understanding of Philippians 1:6 was that the same God who had brought these people to faith in Christ would sustain and nurture them in our absence.

each of those situations. Only a couple of weeks before it was time to leave on our second trip, Terri discovered a lump in her breast. Obviously her health was of utmost concern, so she discussed her decision with her surgeon.

"Should I continue to plan and go to West Africa, or should I stay home and face the options ahead?"

Her doctor, a Christian, responded, "The two weeks that you are gone is not going to change your prognosis one bit. It may change the eternal prognosis of some of the people you will meet on this trip."

Wow.

Terri did go. She spent the time there ministering to the villagers without knowing if this lump was actually cancer or not. If she was overly anxious about the future, it never showed. She gave herself completely to the mission. When she returned home she discovered that she did, in fact, have cancer. She underwent surgery and chemo, and, praise the Lord, she is cancer-free today.

Terri illustrates what many others experience. Rarely has anyone prepared to go on one of our mission journeys without there being a sacrifice involved. For Terri, it meant placing everything in God's hands, denying self, taking up her cross, and following Christ into the village of West Africa. For you the "where" may be different, but it is always about self-denial, taking up our cross, and following Christ wherever He leads us.

Terri had another experience that challenged her, in a much different way, on this same trip. The villagers make a favorite dish out of millet that they call *"toe."* It is gray in color, and much like the texture of playdough, except grittier. What makes it edible is the sauce that they make to dip it in, which can be made out of peanuts, okra, meat (if they have it), or something else handy. Terri had never eaten *toe* before.

One day, as she and a young missions volunteer, Jessica, were walking through the village, greeting some of the women, one of the African women was having a mid-morning snack. She politely offered to share with our ladies. Our people, like all missionaries, are taught to respectfully try the village foods. Terri reached out to pinch off a small bite, but since it was very hot, she quickly drew back her hand. Realizing what happened, the African broke off some in her hand, hawked up a mouth full of spit, and *pittooouie*, spit right into the *toe,* to cool it off.

Jessica leaned over and whispered to Terri, "We have to eat it."

So they did. No one on any of our other journeys has had such an experience, and when I tell other missionaries what happened, they had never seen it happen before. Perhaps a small sacrifice, but still a unique one. And it's a memory that Terri can share with her grandchildren one day.

On this second trip, when we arrived in the village, the new believers I had prayed fervently for—that God would keep secure–were there to greet us with incredible enthusiasm. During the six weeks that we had been away, God had also carried the gospel to a third village and would soon carry it to many more.

As is typical of God's ways, I was learning as much— maybe more than—the new African believers were. Maybe there is a sense in which this mission was more about what God did in our church than it was what He did in West Africa. Our God is able to do *"exceeding abundantly more than we can ever imagine or even ask."*

We often sing *"How Great is Our God"* in church, but are they more than words in our lives? Is our God able to do more than we can dream? Is our God able to do more than we can ever dare to ask Him?

Amazingly, we had started this journey anticipating one or two trips a year. Here I was, however, laughing with new African friends just six weeks after our first-ever international mission trip, as a 200-plus-year-old church. Somehow that seems to me like a pretty amazing start on what has become a God-sized journey into missions.

Retrospect

Every time I share the story of the Africans saying that I was bigger than the donkey, everybody laughs. In Africa, being large is a good thing, so it has never offended me when I am there. Not so much in the U.S. Laughing at me over this comment in our culture would be offensive if not for one important reality. In order to take offense, I have to think more of myself that God gives to me a right to think. The Scriptures are clear that Christ-followers are to die, daily, to self. So if self is dead, how can self be offended? It's not about me. Doesn't self-denial , require us to get over ourselves?

What an incredible day it will be when we, the church, all practice truly dying to self. We will think of Jesus. We will regard others before ourselves. God's Word says, "put off your old self, which belongs to your former manner of life and is corrupt through deceitful desires" (Ephesians 4:22). Then it goes on to say, "put on the new self, created after the likeness of God in true righteousness and holiness" (Ephesians 4:24). Maybe we will learn to recognize that hurt feelings are a warning that the old self is showing up. It can become a signal, not to throw a pity party, but that we need to spend a little time talking to God and allowing His Spirit to help us re-adjust.

The Hardest Job in the World
Chapter 6

"that you may discern what is the will of God,
what is good and acceptable and perfect."
(Romans 12:2d)

The months following my return to God in February of
2004 were a time of incredible spiritual growth and personal
discovery. It was almost as if I had just come to Christ in salvation. Everything was fresh and exciting. Some days I would set
my alarm clock for 5:30 am to get up and have a devotional
time, and I would actually wake at 5. If I set it for 5, then I would
wake up at 4:30. Those morning hours with the Lord were
incredible seasons of refreshment for me.

As I prayed, "God what do You want me to do?" It
seemed like He said, "for now, I want you to pray for others." So
as I renewed acquaintances with old friends, I added them to
my prayer list.

Every morning I would read Psalms and Proverbs. With
the Psalms, I read the date and added thirty. For example, on
the first day of the month, I would read Psalms 1, 31, 61, 91,
121. With the Proverbs, I just read the date. It seemed to me
that Psalms shared with me something of the heart of God and
that Proverbs offered wisdom, and I needed both.

Additionally, I would read through the books of the Old
and New Testament on a reading plan to get through the Bible
in a year.

During the next few months I would visit with the executive director of our denominational state convention, the director of missions of our local denominational association, and many pastors around the state and even the country. A part of me was sensing that God might be calling me back into vocational ministry, but I couldn't believe it. As I talked with others, I was honestly expecting that someone would say, "You cannot do this."

The executive director of the state convention said, "I will be praying God opens the right doors, and if I can help in any way, let me know."

The local associational director of missions said, "I think this is great. Life has changed in the ministry over the last 10 years, so you may need to retool."

Other pastors encouraged me to expect God to work it out.

During this time I traveled to Millington, Tennessee to spend the weekend with a pastor friend and his family. My wife, my youngest daughter, and I had made this trip not knowing what to expect. My friend was letting me preach to the congregation that he served, averaging about 1500 in attendance.

It was like God was saying, "If I want to restore you to the ministry, I can open doors of opportunity larger than you have experienced before."

My friend and I prayed on his patio on that trip, and I remember saying, "Father, if You want me, I will walk through whatever door You open."

It was late summer of that year when I ran into a friend named Buddy that I had met some years earlier but our paths hadn't crossed in a long time. We agreed to get together and discuss what God was doing in each of our lives. We met for lunch on a Friday at a local restaurant. He shared some exciting things about where he was in the Lord, and I told him much of my prodigal story as it is recorded in this book. I leaned up on the table and said, "Buddy, I haven't even told Mitzi, but I am sensing that God may be calling me back into vocational ministry."

Little did I realize how significant that statement or this lunch would prove to be.

The following Thursday my cell phone rang and it was Buddy.

"Have you talked to anyone else from my church?" he asked.

"No," I replied, "why do you ask?"

"Our pastor resigned last night," he said.

"Is that a positive thing or a negative thing for the church," I asked.

"Probably neutral," was the response.

"Well, that is interesting," I continued, "and with no disrespect intended, Buddy, what does that have to do with me?"

I sensed his call had a purpose other than simply providing me updates on his church's life.

"Brad," he said, "I am the chairman of deacons, and I believe God wants you to be the next pastor."

Honestly caught by surprise, I asked, "Do the deacons make that choice for the church?"

"No, not exactly," he said. "The deacons choose the interim pastor, and the chairman of the deacons nominates someone for the deacons to consider. I have called the associational office and asked for resumes, and I was wondering if they have yours."

"They do," I replied.

I became their interim pastor late in 2004. Then, in August of 2005, I was called as pastor.

During the interim time my wife and I were still owners of a sign company, which continued to take a significant amount of my time. Finally, in the summer of 2005, God provided a buyer, bringing that chapter of my life came to a close. I was once again free to devote myself to serving as a pastor full time.

It was while I was serving as interim pastor that someone I knew through our sign business said to me, "I hear you are going back into the ministry. Is that right?"

"That is right."

Continuing, he said," Being a pastor must be the hardest job in the world."

"Actually, it is not," I responded.

"Then, what is?" he asked.

"The hardest job in the world," I said, "is trying to do something different from what God wants you to do. The most fulfilling and rewarding job, and therefore, the easiest job in the world to do is the one that God created you for."

As I served the church as interim pastor I found myself mulling over the question, *So, what do you do with a church that is over 200 years old?*" The church had started in 1806, while

Thomas Jefferson was President of the United States. Obviously that means there is a lot of tradition, and a danger perhaps of falling into a mindset that relives past glory—the good old days. My previous experience as pastor had been in starting a brand new church and building from scratch. There had been a couple of years in bi-vocational ministry, but I don't count that because, honestly, I was still too far from being surrendered to God during that time.

The director of missions for our local Baptist association had advised me that I might need to retool. Eventually that would mean continuing my doctoral studies, but initially it meant doing a lot of reading. What I soon discovered was that the world had changed over the last 13 years. That seems so obvious when I say it, but in ministry, we are often too slow to recognize change around us.

I remember hearing an illustration of a frog placed in a pot of water on the stove. If you put a pot on the stove and let the water boil, toss in a frog, it will jump out. But if you place the pot on the stove with lukewarm water and the frog already in it, you can gradually heat it until it cooks to death. I can't think of anything yummier than boiled frog, can you? *Yuuuucccccck.* Being thrust back into ministry after 13 years in secular business, I was much like that frog tossed into scalding hot water. Indeed I could tell that things were much different than what my seminary training had prepared me for. At the same time, many folks inside the church were doing the same old things without realizing that the climate of ministry had changed. They were like the frog gradually being heated on top of the stove. The church does not get the same results that the methods once produced. But now that they are failing methodologies, it makes no sense to continue to do the same things. While the illustration may break down ultimately, my point is the frog in the kettle is unaware that his environment is changing until it is too late. The frog dies without realizing what is happening.

One of the messages I began to challenge our leadership with, and ultimately the church with, is the recognition that if we keep doing what we have always done, we will keep getting the same results that we have always gotten. We resist change, because we are uncomfortable with change, and we keep doing what we have always done.

Sometimes I hear people emphasize words such as "liberal" and "conservative" methodologies, and I don't understand it. We talk about contemporary methodologies as though they are automatically liberal, or even compromised. We suggest that a church is liberal because it doesn't sing the old hymns and preach from the King James Version of the Bible.

Let me state my point of view very clearly. I believe that God's message never changes. The Bible teaches that we have a sin problem. The Bible teaches that Jesus Christ is God's perfect provision for our sins. The Bible teaches that the only way we have access to the Father is through Jesus Christ. The Bible teaches that each person is responsible to repent of his or her sins and place their trust in Jesus Christ. The message never changes.

But the methodology of communicating that message must constantly change. The cultural context and the current circumstances challenge us to find methodologies that communicate truth to the present generation without compromising the Word of God. Some of what members of the church I served would call traditional music was actually the contemporary music of the day in which they grew up.

As I study the book of Acts, I am impressed with the organic and dynamic nature of the church. The early church was not perfect and they made mistakes. At the same time, they relied on the Holy Spirit to guide them in ministry in each circumstance and context. As Jesus ascended back to heaven He told the early believers to wait in Jerusalem until the promise of the Holy Spirit's indwelling Presence was fulfilled. In much the same way that God had breathed life into Adam and he became a living being, on the day of Pentecost, God the Holy Spirit breathed life into this band of disciples and they became a living church. Reading through the book of Acts, you cannot conclude the church is some finely tuned organization. It is a body of followers of Jesus Christ that comprise a living organism and the life-breath of that organism is the Holy Spirit.

If God is the same today as He was yesterday (Hebrews 13:8), it makes perfect sense that the church should continually follow the direction of the Holy Spirit and develop its ministries in accordance with the directing orders of the Spirit of God. Without His guidance the very best we can do is imitate some other church that is having success in a context similar to ours. If that is our approach, let's be honest, we will only have what people can do in their own strength and by their own abilities.

I want to see something happen in the church and community where God has placed me that cannot be explained by the sum total of the resources and talents of the membership of our body. I want to see something happen that can only be explained with the words, "God did it."

Recognizing that "God is the same" does not mean that we lock ourselves into methodologies of the past. God is organic. He is alive. Our methodologies have to take the unchanging message and communicate in the cultural language of our field of service.

Ed Stetzer and David Putnam have called effectiveness in communicating in our cultural context a result of "breaking the missional code."[6] They say that we must be missional to reach our communities by sharing the gospel message and that "involves understanding them before we tell them."

Retrospect

Shortly after I had been called as pastor, my friend from Millington, Tennessee, called, so I asked him, "Steve, has God told you to share anything with me about the work He has called me to?"

"Interesting that you ask that question, Brad," Steve replied. "Indeed He has."

"So, what did He say to tell me?" My curiosity was sufficiently aroused.

Steve then replied, "He asked me to remind you that people don't really care how much you know until they know how much you care."

[6] Stetzer, Ed and David Putnam, 2006; *Breaking the Missional Code.* Nashville, Tenn., Broadman and Holman Publishers; p. 2-3.

After one year as interim pastor, the church voted to extend the call to me as their full-time pastor. The vote was just over 75% affirmative, which means that nearly one-fourth of those voting were opposed. By the way, the bylaws required a 75% confirmation to be called. No doubt I had ruffled a few feathers during my interim. However, I think all pastors know that neither a unanimous call, nor a minimum show of support, is indicative of what is truly to come.

Compassion may well be the greatest apologetic that we have for our faith. No matter where God enables any believer to serve, our message will never be any louder than our love is real.

Working in West Africa has helped me learn this. In that culture, relationship is everything. You can never minister there without first building relational bridges to people.

Because of the value placed on relationships, people are far more important than schedule and being on time. Someone has said, "God gave the Americans watches, and He gave the Africans time." We need to rediscover in Western culture that people matter more than programs. Relationships are more significant that maintaining schedules. People don't care how much we know if they do not know how much we care.

New Believers in Christ
Chapter 7

*Therefore, if anyone is in Christ, he is a new creation.
The old has passed away; behold, the new has come.*
(2 Corinthians 5:17)

Where do you begin to make disciples of brand new believers in a culture where any and everything Christian is essentially different from anything they have ever known? That was the task presented to us after making the decision to adopt a village among this people group. When we left Africa in February of 2007, as far as we knew there were now between 12 and 15 believers in two small villages where the name of Jesus had not been before.

In much of West Africa, a person's identity is intricately tied to his extended family. His cousins are as close as brothers. He'll call his uncle "father." And his family members will be the ones who help him when he needs money to send his kids to school or to buy millet when his crops fail. He'll live with extended family his whole life.

Shame and respect, too, carry a great deal of significance to these people. "Saving face" has higher value than telling the truth. Respecting one's elders, especially one's parents, is paramount.

Both those aspects of their culture are useful in the first lesson we taught the new believers.

The focal passage of Scripture was John 1:12, "*But to all who did receive Him, who believed in His name, He gave the right to become children of God."* The object of this first lesson was to help the new believers understand that they were now a part of the family of God and how they should treat God as their Father and learn to respect Him. Additionally, we wanted them to be assured of the love God had for them and His ability to meet their needs.

As we began I said, "I want to tell you a story that comes from the Word of God. This is not a story that is made up by men, but it is a true story from the Bible. One of the first followers of Jesus was named John. As an old man he wrote down his experience of following Jesus in a book called the Gospel of John. In that book, John tells us that everyone who receives Jesus as their Lord and Savior become children of God. Not everyone received Jesus and welcomed Jesus. Those who chose to be His followers became a part of His family. This is a story that comes from God's Word."

"Do you have any questions about this story?" I asked.

"Ai – ee (No)", they said in unison.

"Then I would like to ask you some questions. Would that be alright?" I asked.

"O-wo (Yes), that would be alright," they replied.

"What do you expect from your children?" I began.

"We expect our children to obey us, and show respect," one volunteered.

"That's great," I said. "What are some of the ways that your children show you respect?"

"They greet us properly in the mornings," one said.

"They deliver messages to the other side of the village, or to other villages, when we need them to," another added.

"They obey our instructions, "someone said.

"Thanks for sharing these things with me, can you think of any other ways you expect them to show you proper respect?" I asked one more time.

They talked among themselves for a moment, and finally one spoke for the group and said, "We expect them to listen to us, and learn the ways of our people."

"Very good," I added.

"That is all we can think of," one chimed in.

"This is all very good," I told them. "We have seen in our Bible story today that when we become a follower of Jesus Christ, we become a part of His family. God becomes our Father. Our heavenly Father wants us to show Him honor and the proper respect, just like we want our children to do for us."

African heads were nodding, and they were giving the guttural "uh-huh" affirmations typical to them. I love sharing bible stories and training in West Africa because you have no doubt when they are listening and when they are not. I have managed to put them to sleep there as well as I do here.

"You said that one of the ways you expect your children to show you the proper respect is by greeting you when they get up in the mornings. Is that correct?"

"Ah-wo (Yes)."

"How would you feel in the morning if your children got out of bed and went and greeted the neighbors and began to play with their friends, but totally ignored you?" I asked.

"We would not like that," one said.

"I would feel disrespected," said another.

"In the same way," I said, "our heavenly Father wants us to greet Him first in the morning. We can do that through prayer. Not the ritualistic prayers that the Muslims pray where you memorize words in a language you do not understand. But in the conversational prayers that we taught you when you first became a Jesus follower."

Their eyes were focused on me and they were listening very carefully.

"How do you think God feels if we begin our day by greeting others, but not Him. Or if we rush into the matters of our day without talking to Him first?" I asked.

"I don't think that He would like it very much."

"I think He would feel disrespected, just like we do when our children do that," said another.

"What do you think God wants you to do, then?" I asked.

"He wants us to begin our day by greeting Him proper-ly," several said.

"Will you do that?" I asked.

"O-wo (yes)," they all replied.

"Another thing that you told me you expect of your children," I continued, "is that they listen to you and learn the ways of your people."

"Uh-huh" they said.

"God our heavenly Father wants that of His children, as well. He wants us to listen to the things that He says. He speaks to us through His Word, the Bible," I said. "God wants to talk with us everyday. Those of you who can read should read to those who cannot," I continued. "Will you do that?"

"O-wo (yes)," they replied.

"And we have given many of you the mega-voices[7] with many of God's stories on them. Continue to listen to them everyday," I said.

"Just like you want your children to learn the ways of your people, God wants you to learn the ways of being a Jesus follower," I continued. "You also said that you give your children messages to deliver to other people in the village, or even in other villages," I said. "Is that correct?"

"O-wo (yes)," they said.

"God has given to us a message to deliver to all the people in our villages, and to all the other villages around us, " I said. "God has asked us as His children to tell everyone else about Him and how they can follow Jesus. If your children do not deliver your messages," I asked, "How do you feel?"

"Disrespected."

"Disappointed."

"Angry."

"I am sure that God must feel the same way when we don't deliver His message," I said.

"One more thing that you did not mention," I said. "In my country we expect our children to participate in gatherings that the family has together."

One of the Africans spoke up quickly, "It is the same way here."

"Well, it is also the same way in God's family," I said. "God delights in us having regular family gatherings, where we

---

[7] These are small solar powered recorders that have 60 bible stories on them. They are available in many different languages from *God's Story*. http://www.gods-story.org

honor Him and help one another. In the Bible we read about the first followers of Jesus meeting in each other's homes daily, and gathering regularly for celebration with everyone. When can you meet together at least weekly?"

There was some discussion among the Africans, and then one spoke for the group, "We will meet at 9 on Sunday morning."

"What about the women," I asked. "Can they come that early?"

"No, they will not be finished their morning work," someone said.

"Do you think that God would want them to meet with you?"

"O-wo (yes)," several replied together.

"So when is a better time to meet, that will include them," I asked.

After another lengthy discussion, they announced, "We will meet on Sunday mornings at 10:30."

"Let me tell you this story one more time," I said. "This is a story from the Word of God," I said, and then repeated the story one more time. Believe it or not, through the translator, this took about 45 minutes.

As we prepared to end this training session, I asked, "What do you think that God would have you do with this story in your own life?"

We went around the circle and let each person share his or her application. Then I asked, "Who do you know that needs to hear this story?"

Each one gave their answers.

"When will you tell them," I asked.

After each had responded, we had prayer for them to apply the lesson and to share the lesson.

"When we gather again, "I said, "I will let you share how you have made progress applying the lesson and telling the story to others."

Retrospect

In my first book, *The Gospel Unleashed*[8], I describe this training methodology as *participative discipleship*. The process works well in any culture, and is taught in *T4T: A Discipleship ReRevolution*.[9] It should be our objective to evangelize the lost, especially where the gospel has never been proclaimed, and we should make disciples of those who respond, giving them the tools to live a victorious meaningful life in Christ. The objective is not only to transfer information, but to train trainers who will train others so that a movement begins. As disciples are made they will mature and form churches.

---

[8] *The Gospel Unleashed* by Brad Bessent. Available at this link: http://www.amazon.com/Gospel-Unleashed-Releasing-Acts-Church/dp/1500701602/ref=sr_1_1?ie=UTF8&qid=1415380450&sr=8-1&keywords=the+gospel+unleashed
[9] Ying Kai and Steve Smith, *T4T:A Discipleship ReRevolution*. (Bangalore, India: Wigtake Resources, 2011.

Don't Give Me the God-Answer
Chapter 8

"Now to Him Who is able to do far more abundantly than all we ask or think, according to the power at work within us."
(Ephesians 3:20)

The event was called a "West Africa Summit." Missionaries and churches engaged in mission partnerships would be offering training on how to do mission work in West Africa to churches throughout our denomination. Because we were sending teams every six weeks from our church, and because we are not a mega-church, I had been invited to share a testimony of what God was doing through our average-sized church and to lead a couple of break-out sessions from a pastor's perspective.

In one of the break-out sessions I shared that the average cost for someone going on one of our trips was about $4,000, if it was their first trip. In addition to the airline tickets, first-timers would need a passport and visa, along with a number of vaccinations and shots. Some additional in-country expenses also contributed to the hefty cost. I told the group that none of the funds had been taken from our church budget.

One of the participants raised his hand, and asked, "How have you done this?" Then he added," And don't give me the God-answer."

"May I have the next question," I said.

"Wait," he objected, "You didn't answer my question."

I smiled and said, "Sir, you took away the only answer that I can give you."

There is absolutely no other answer to the question of "how." The church that I served is located in a semi-rural community on the outskirts of the capital of our state. It is a lower middle-income

blue-collar community. Although this church has been predominantly a white church throughout its history, the community is predominantly African-American. With a history of 200 plus years under our belt, you can imagine that traditions are important. Like many other churches in our denomination, we were mission minded. We gave a significant amount of money to our denomination's home and international mission agencies and we prayed for missionaries. Occasionally our young people participated in mission projects to do things like Vacation Bible Schools or to repair roofs. They had once traveled on such a trip to Australia. What I am trying to say is that there is no human explanation for how we have become a participant on the international mission scene.

As the new pastor, I was continually praying that God would lead me in developing His vision for the church. Early in 2006, I attended a one-day pastor's coaching network conference hosted by a friend of mine. I went because he asked me to go. One of the break-out sessions at this conference featured short-term international mission trips. An international missionary, a denominational employee from our state convention, and two pastors led this session. I left with a sense of conviction in my heart that our church should be doing more than praying and giving money to missions.

I scheduled a conference with the state denominations mission coordinator. She shared with me some of the ways that we could become involved more directly.

I sent an email to someone I knew at our denomination's international mission board office. He responded that he was out of the country but would have someone contact me. Actually two different people made contact with me, Larry and Mike. We decided to meet in June at our annual denominational meeting held in Greensboro, NC.

We sat down in a coffee shop at the convention center. Because I had forgotten to bring a notepad, we ended up drawing up a strategy for our church on the back of a hotel's stationery envelope. That was where it began in earnest for our church.

Returning home, my first two steps were to preach on our God-ordained responsibility in missions, and to form a Global Impact Team. We held our first meeting on a Monday night towards the end of July, 2006. I invited anyone who would be interested in learning more about how we as a church could become more missional to a supper meeting. It was a free meal, and approximately 35 people showed up. Larry from the IMB came to lead the meeting. After we ate, he addressed the group.

"There are two things that I would suggest we attempt to accomplish tonight. First, I encourage you to come up with a definition of missions for your church. Secondly, I think you should determine what Acts 1:8 means for your church."

We sat at the round tables in our fellowship hall and worked in groups of 6 to 8. As we compiled the results, we came up with this synopsis: "For our church, missions will be about either planting churches or assisting churches, and it must engage lostness."

The second question of how we would understand Acts 1:8 was answered in this way: "Jerusalem will represent our immediate community; Judea will be North America; Samaria will represent crossing cultural boundaries in the US (such as prison ministry, crossing ethnic lines, ministering to the homeless, or something that took us out of working with people just like us); and the ends of the earth will be international mission work."

We passed a notepad around the room and asked people to choose which area they were most interested in, and to give a second choice. I proposed that since the church had been working on our Jerusalem for over 200 years that we address the other end of the equation first. Larry told the group that he would come back in a couple of weeks and lead us in the next step.

He said, "I am going to leave this map of the world hanging here, and I suggest that you pray about what part of the world, and keep looking at the map and see if God leads your eyes to keep returning to the same place."

Larry did return in a couple of weeks, but I missed that meeting. I had gotten up that morning with a pain in a very delicate place that prevented me from sitting comfortably. So I had gone to my family doctor who had referred me to another specialist. (My dad used to call that, "sharing the wealth.")

The specialist said, "I need to do a little surgical procedure."

"When?" I asked,

"How much does it hurt?" he asked.

"A lot," I answered."

He smiled and said, "I suggest we do it right now." As he performed his little "surgical procedure" I told him that I had a very important meeting that night I could not miss.

"You won't want to go to that," he responded.

"Not only do I want to go to that," I said, "I have to go to that."

Totally unmoved by my urgent pleas for his approval to attend the meeting he said, "Trust me, you don't want to go to that meeting."

"OK, I will play along," I said. "Where will I want to be?"

"You, sir," he answered, "will want to be at home soaking in a hot tub of water with Epsom salts."

I know, TMI (too much information) but I wanted you to understand I was not at the next meeting, even though I really wanted to be there to see what would happen.

The group that met that night decided God was leading us to work somewhere in West Africa.

At the time we began this journey, our international mission board had the world divided into geographical regions. They have subsequently reorganized around affinity groups of peoples.

When we decided West Africa, however, we were just getting started on where. West Africa was comprised of approximately 22 countries and covered a physical expanse roughly equivalent to the size of the continental United States.

"So now what do we do?" I asked Larry on the telephone a couple of days later.

"There is a West Africa summit being held in St. Charles, Missouri in November," he said, "why don't you attend that?"

Five of us attended that summit. Accompanying me to St. Charles were: one of our deacons, Mason; his wife, Priscilla; another deacon, Terry; and 17-year-old Jessica.

We heard missionaries from different people groups speak and we learned something of the methodologies of working in West Africa.

At that time, there was a director of Baptist mission work in West Africa named Randy. We cornered him one day and said, "We need to talk with you. We want to help you in West Africa. Where do you need us?"

Over the next two days, Randy and two other missionaries, Marvin and Jeff, met with our group and eventually gave us four different people groups to pray about working with. They even listed them in the order of priority from their perspective. We discovered that three of the people groups were in the country of Mali, and so we determined to go on a vision trip there as soon as possible to visit those people groups and see what happened.

On a practical side, that is how it happened for us. When we returned home, we began praying, "Lord, who should go on this vision trip? When do we go?"

Mason and Terry, who had attended the summit felt led to go,. Marvin joined us, and the team was set. We communicated with field personnel in Mali, and chose to plan for

February, 2007.The four of us began the process of securing passports, visas, and raising money to go.

These details may seem mundane, but it is important to understand that prayer and faith guided this whole process. We believed that God knew where He wanted us to work as a church and we knew He would tell us where, if we would seek Him in prayer. There is no answer other than the "God-answer."

Sometimes I hear people say something like this, "Well, the way I see God is . . ."

Others are so bold as to say, "My God is like . . ."

Do we honestly think that God is whatever we want to make Him? God is not Who we make Him out to be. A god of our own imagination would be formed in our image, rather than being a Creator Who formed us in His image. There is a biblical word for recreating a god in our image. It is called idolatry and it wholly condemned in Scripture.

When Moses was tending sheep on the backside of the desert for his father-in-law, he saw a bush burning on the side of the mountain, but it was not being consumed. As he approached that sight, God spoke, telling him to take off his sandals because he stood on holy ground. In the ensuing conversation Moses dared to ask God to tell him His name.

"God said to Moses, 'I am Who I am.'"(Exodus 3:14).

God spoke one word as His name, YHWH. The Hebrew language does not have vowels. Because there was a long period of time where the Jewish people thought it too irreverent to speak God's name out loud, they eventually forgot how to pronounce it. So English scholars eventually supplied vowels from the Hebrew name, Adonai, and came up with Jehovah, and later, Yahweh. This one word is written as the present tense of the verb "to be." That literally would be, *"I AM"*. As eternal present tense it would mean, *"I was, I am, I will be."*

God is Who He is, not who we want, or try and make Him. Too often the modern Western church and its people have reduced God to a size that we think we can manage or manipulate. We build our plans and set our goals around things that we know we can accomplish whether God shows up or not.

We are learning in West Africa that our God is a great and mighty God. He is far bigger and greater than we could ever conceive. He is immeasurable, without beginning or end. He is uncontainable, holding this vast expansive universe in the very palm of His hand. He can do anything He wants to do. I believe that God is exactly like He has revealed Himself to be in the Scripture, except that He is even greater than the words on the pages of Scripture can express.

At a subsequent conference a couple of years later I related this story. At lunchtime a man tapped me on the shoulder and when I turned around he asked, "Do you know me?"

I replied, "You look familiar, but I am not sure."

He said, "I am the man who asked you that question a couple of years ago. I have since been on a mission trip to West Africa since that summit. Now I know exactly what you mean."

There really is no answer *but* the God-answer. Wouldn't it be wonderful if that was true of everything the church does? Don't you want to be a part of something bigger and greater than the sum total of the skills and resources of the people in the congregation where you attend church?

I do.

Retrospect

Is there anything happening in your life that cannot be explained by your own human ability and resources?

A good friend of mine was telling me several years ago that he called his church to a solemn assembly on Sunday morning. He had preached through the book of Joel, the prophet who called God's people to fast and pray and seek God. *"Consecrate a fast; call a solemn assembly. Gather the elders and all the inhabitants of the land to the house of the LORD your God, and cry out to the LORD."* (Joel 1:14)

In a deacon's meeting prior to that Sunday, the men asked, "Pastor, what are we going to do in this 'solemn assembly'?"

The pastor replied, "We are going to read Scripture for about 45 minutes to an hour and then we are going to turn the service over to God."

"What is your back-up plan?" someone asked.

I wonder if one of the reasons that we don't often see God do anything out of the ordinary in the 21st century Western Church is the fact that we always have a back-up plan.

We cry out to God in prayer, but then, just in case He doesn't answer, we come up with our contingency agenda. As if we have to protect God, in case He cannot do anything. Ridiculous!

God is not to be mocked or to put to the test to suit our appetite for the strange or unusual. God is capable, however, of keeping up His side of any promise He has made. Throughout the Scriptures, God often demonstrates His power to do what otherwise could never be done.

We will never see God act in a supernatural way if we plan everything on the basis of what we can accomplish without His help. Imagine Elijah setting up an altar to have a showdown between Baal and Yahweh in a 21st century Western church. Dare we call on God to answer with fire? How would Joshua dare to pray that the sun stand still in a church committee meeting? Can we cross the flooded Jordan River expecting the waters to part? Or march around Jericho anticipating the walls to collapse? What would a Resurrection do to the cemetery committee's budget?

God doesn't seem to involve Himself in any miraculous way when we are self-sufficient. Miracles are not a spectator sport for the amusement of the crowds. God does what only God can do when it declares His glory and accomplishes His purpose. Can God supply the finances for an individual to go on a mission trip? Can God raise up team members for the trip? Can a church with an average attendance of 150—or less for that matter—send a team to West Africa every 6 to 8 weeks? Can God revive a lethargic church? Can God change the hearts of people that are not concerned about a lost world? God can obviously do whatever He wants to do when He wants to do it. Let's give the God-answer every time.

God Did This
Chapter 9

"And a vision appeared to Paul in the night:
a man of Macedonia was standing there, urging him and
saying, 'Come over to Macedonia and help us.'" (Acts 16:9)

As the rain beat down on the tin roof of our mud hut, five of us huddled inside, singing praise to God.

"How Great is our God, sing with me, how great is our God, and all will see..."

Between the litany of songs—the parts we could remember—we offered prayers for the remainder of our team who were somewhere between the capital city and our village.

It was August, 2007, and trip number 3 for me and Mason, and trip number 1 for Andy. Jessica had been in Mali since January, staying the whole year assisting some of the missionaries. We had a Malian translator, who was a believer, along with us. This was the fourth trip a team from our church had made into the village and five of our team were missing the first day. Ryan and Sarah, from another church, along with Shannon from our church, were on their first trip. Our driver and a female translator were with them, and because of the rain they had not yet made it to the village.

Partly because of the rain, and partly because we only had one vehicle to get everyone to the village—my effort to save money. So the veterans—Mason, Jessica, our translator, and I—along with rookie, Andy, had gone out to set up our mission post at the hut.

It was the first time I had seen the hut, which was built between trips 2 and 3. I didn't make trip 3, and both of my trips had been during dry seasons, when the landscape was brown and dusty. I could hardly believe I was in the same place, as the trees were green and all types of vegetation had sprung up.

The dirt road to the village was almost completely under water. Some high parts of the dirt showed, but it still looked like a river winding through the bush country. Our four-wheel drive had served us well on the way out and the driver managed to avoid being stuck, but it had been a difficult journey.

Arriving in the village around midday we unloaded and immediately dispatched the driver back to pick up the remainder of our team. We set up for the week, assembling our water filter, placing chairs out under the hangar—a thatch-covered shaded area on the front of the hut. The hut itself is about 16 feet wide and 8 feet deep with a wall down the middle separating it into two rooms. On the back of the hut there are two windows to each room, and on the front one door to each. The floor is a very thin layer of concrete. The walls are made of mud bricks covered with a thin layer of dirt mixed with some concrete. The roof is a supported by wooden beams and covered by tin, which oddly tilts to the front of the house instead of the rear, causing all of the water to run off toward the doors.

Late afternoon it began to rain. If you have ever seen the movie, *Forest Gump*, there is a scene where they are on patrol in Viet Nam and he talks about the rain coming from every direction. That describes very well what happens in the bush of Mali. Sitting inside the hut listening to the rain pummeling the roof is an experience hard to describe. It comes down with such force you think, it couldn't rain any harder than that, but then it does. So now you are convinced it is pouring as hard as it can, and it ramps up even more. Peaking out our slightly opened front door, the dirt road beside our house looked like the rapids in a river. As dark approached it became more and more obvious that the remainder of our team would not likely make the village.

As we were singing we heard a *"moto"*, a chain-driven moped that is a favorite form of transportation for those who can manage to afford one, winding its way toward the village. We laughed inside our hut at the craziness of someone riding through this weather and down the river of a road. Suddenly it stopped in front of our hut, and we opened the door.

A drenched villager handed us a note that had been folded inside a plastic bag. The message said, *"Pray for us, we've got a little problem. Ryan is cut up real bad. Shannon is OK."* Any slight anxiety I had felt was immediately replaced by outright concern. What had happened? Did they run off the road and hit a tree? Was Ryan seriously injured to the point of being in danger? Where were they?

Did I mention that the village does not have electricity or running water? Oddly enough they have a coke machine in the center of the village powered by a generator. We had purchased a satellite phone and now was the time to test it out. I called the city and got our missionary partner on the phone. I said, *"Steve, something has happened to part of our team,"* and I read him the note.

Steve laughed and said, "We have already heard from them. They are fine . . . but they are stuck and won't make it tonight. Marvin, my supervisor, and I are headed out in my truck to tow them out of the mud. Just don't expect them tonight."

I was certainly relieved to discover that they were safe and sound, but now I was concerned that this experience will have upset them so much that they might want to go home as soon as they get here.

The rain stops about as fast as it starts during rainy season in Mali. We stretched out a plastic tarp on the ground in front of the hut, and set up mosquito tents under the star-filled sky. We prayed and decided to get a good night's sleep. I couldn't help but think that the devil had disrupted this trip already; however, the next morning I would have a different perspective.

We finished breakfast and were preparing to prayer-walk the village when two vehicles drove up. One was our Land Cruiser with the rest of our team, and the other was the truck with the missionaries.

I thought, What encouraging words can I say that will save this trip for our rescued team mates?

Ryan, Sarah, and Shannon jumped out of the vehicle and all began to talk at once with an obvious enthusiasm that soon caught on with us. "The most incredible thing has happened. We spent the night in a new village. The villagers were incredible to us. They wanted to hear all about what we were doing and why we are here. They want us to come back. Can we go back, Brad? When can we go back? We have got to tell them the stories!"

They were all talking at once, and I was trying to comprehend it all.

Finally, Ryan said, "Brad, the Muslim chief in the village said this to me as we prepared to leave. 'We watched your team drive by our village all year long. We knew that you had good news to share, but you didn't stop and tell us. We prayed to God, and He has stopped you here that we might hear your story. Some of our elders remember that there were Christians who came here long ago. They said that they knew the Christians had the truth of God's Word, but we have not heard it. You must come back and share this message with us.'"

Did you do this, God? Why hadn't we taken the time to stop and at least greet these villagers? How could we have been so task-focused—so American—to stay on our schedule, that we had been blind to this village? How could I have thought the devil had sidetracked our team? Thank you God, for giving us this opportunity and for being patient with us while we figure this entire mission out.

Our African Daughter

On this same trip we wanted to teach the new believers about the observance of the Lord's Supper. Several times during the week we taught the stories of the Passover meal that Jesus shared with his disciples. We taught how Jesus had transformed the Old Testament remembrance of the delivery of God's people from Egyptian bondage into a meaningful reminder of His deliverance of believers from bondage to sin by His death on the cross. We had explained the symbolism of the cup and the bread.

On Saturday, we asked, "How can you observe this meal? What can you use for the elements of the Lord's Supper?"

The believers had a discussion among themselves, and then reported to us, "We will use little millet cakes for the bread, and we have a red tea we can use for the cup."

"That's a great idea," I said. "Will you guys make all the arrangements for that?"

"We will," they said.

These elements certainly fit the first principle I had learned about mission strategy of utilizing a reproducible strategy. The believers in our village couldn't go to the market and buy grape juice in their village. Neither could they go to the Christian bookstore in the mall to purchase communion wafers. Millet cakes and red tea are very Malian. This is another way we work to allow an *African church* to emerge from our teaching of God's Word, instead of trying to reproduce a copy of our American churches.

During the Sunday morning worship service before we shared the Lord's Supper, I was preaching a message on *heaven*. One of the things that I said was that heaven is a wonderful place where there is no more sickness or disease. There is no more pain and suffering. A young girl of the village tapped Shannon on the shoulder during my message, and rolled up her sleeve revealing a large abscess at her elbow that literally went all the way to the bone. Even though the missionaries had told us that it was inappropriate to cry in public among this people group, Shannon could not contain it and began to weep. To our surprise many of the women of the village that were present also began to weep.

Steve had driven out for the first observance of the Lord's Supper with our villagers. After the worship service we discussed the situation with this young girl's arm. Her name is Hawa, which translates "Eve". We decided that we would take her back into the city and find out what needed to be done to treat her. When we discussed this with her, Hawa began to cry. As we asked her why she was upset, she said, "I want to be baptized first."

She told us that getting help for her arm would not mean anything if she could not be baptized and show the others in her village that she was going to follow Jesus. That afternoon, Hawa was baptized along with several others, and then she went to the city with the missionary to see the doctor.

What an incredible day it had become. The Lord's Supper and baptism all on the same day in this village where just a few months earlier, they had never heard the name of Jesus.

We spent most of our time on this trip in F-village, with a couple of day trips to B-village and D-village, where the gospel had already been shared. Mason, the male translator and myself stayed in F-village for the last night of training with the believers here.

We sent part of our team---Ryan, Sarah, Shannon, and Andy, along with the female translator--to N-village for the last night in the bush, and a handful of villagers became followers of Christ.

One of the men there was named "Baba", as in Ali Baba and the 40 thieves. Ryan and Andy were sleeping in Baba's hut.

About 4:45 am, Baba crept over to Ryan's bed and shook him to wake him up. Baba had learned a word the night before, "Babatize". And as he shook Ryan, he kept repeating, *"Babatize, Babatize."* Ryan pushed the button on the side of his digital watch that lit it enough to show the time, and then he pointed to the watch, making sign language of some form to suggest Baba go back to sleep. Baba smiled, nodded approvingly and laid back down….for 15 minutes. At 6 am he was pulling Ryan out of bed, repeating again, "Babatize, babatize."

Ryan put his shoes on, grabbed a flashlight, and the two headed down a path to a watering hole. It was rainy season. These water holes are not there most of the year.

The two men waded into the water, and saying words he had said in America before, knowing the African didn't know what he was saying, Ryan baptized Baba in the early morning hours of that Wednesday in August, 2007.

When we picked them up on the way out to the paved road, Mason and I met the new friends in N-village. Praying with them we promised that our future teams would at least stop and offer encouragement on our way in and out.

As we made our way home from that trip, I reflected on what God had taught me. *"Firm flexibility"* is what I decided to call it. We would continue to map out strategy for each trip. We would continue to focus on discipling the believers in F-village in order to entrust the responsibility of spreading the gospel to those believers.

At the same time, however, we would remember to be more sensitive to the promptings of the Holy Spirit and to the "roadblocks" God orchestrated so that we did not miss any real

God-moments. In Acts 16, Paul ran into some roadblocks as he sought to carry out his strategy. Then in a vision a man from Macedonia appeared and said, *"Come over to Macedonia, and help us."* (Acts 16:9, ESV).

I remember thinking, How awesome is this? We are not just reading about the events of the Bible anymore, we are living them out.

Retrospect

Mason accompanied me on all three of my first trips to West Africa. He would go a number of times after this and even accompany me on a trip to Peru. Mason is the out-front spokesman of the crowd. Often when we were in West Africa, however, I would be teaching and look around to see Mason caught up in prayer. He definitely has a servant's heart.

If I am the donkey—an idea that seemed quite popular among my friends and family, *usually* in jest—let me suggest that Mason be dubbed, along with others in our churches, a "donkey fetcher."

In all four gospels we encounter the story of Jesus' triumphal entry into Jerusalem, riding a donkey as the people cry "*Hosanna*". In Matthew 21:1-3 we read, "*Now when they drew near to Jerusalem and came to Bethphage, to the Mount of Olives, then Jesus sent two disciples, saying to them, "Go into the village in front of you, and immediately you will find a donkey tied, and a colt with her. Untie them and bring them to Me. If anyone says anything to you, you shall say, 'The Lord needs them,' and he will send them at once."*

I don't know which two disciples Jesus dispatched with this assignment. I do know that there was nothing glamorous about it. Perhaps if given this assignment some of us would be inclined to say, "Lord, that is not what I signed on for. I have weathered the storms on the sea of Galilee with You, I have accompanied You on some long hard roads, and I am willing to learn to be a fisher of men, but fetching donkeys is not really my thing."

Donkey-fetchers are those servant-hearted people in the body of Christ that do whatever Jesus needs them to do. They don't need credit or public applause. They don't complain that they are taken advantage of or unappreciated. They just quietly and faithfully give service "as unto the Lord, and not to people." (Colossians 3:17) Let me say thank you to those like my friend Mason who serve so well and often behind the scenes.

Don't Beat the Donkeys
Chapter 10

*"And the donkey said to Balaam, 'What have I done to you,
that you have struck me these three times?'
(Numbers 22:28b)*

One of the things that struck me in the village life of
West Africa was how abusive the people seemed to be to their
donkeys. Little children have sticks and at times absolutely wail
the tar out of the side of one of the donkeys trying to get them
to do what they want. The children learned it from the parents
who learned it from their grandparents, and so on back to the
day they got off the ark I am sure.

One of the other things that I have been amazed by
is the ineffectiveness of that process. The donkeys have been
trained to do certain tasks, such as pull carts, or haul bags of
millet, and for the most part seem to comply with the routines
they have been trained to follow. Every so often, however, it
seems appropriate to one of the Africans to take their sticks
and just lay a wallop or two on the donkey. By and large, it
seems to me to have very little effect in changing their behavior.

A number of years ago I had a friend who pastored a
church in the same association as me. His name was Charles,
although everyone called him Buddy. Buddy told me one day
that if he screamed and yelled for 20 to 30 minutes during
sermon time the folks in church would go out the door saying,
"Pastor, that was a great sermon today, we really needed that."

"But," he said, "if I spend my time teaching them something with content, they think I have become liberal and stopped preaching."

The quality of the sermon seemed to be measured by the volume, the sweating and spitting, and the amount of scolding that was given out. The only problem with that is it is like beating the donkey. It really doesn't result in life change. Psychologically it may have some cathartic effect to relieve guilt, but after church, folks are back to doing the same sins they were doing before they came.

Working in an oral culture has required us to learn methods more geared toward "training" than "teaching". We discussed that already in a previous chapter. I return to this subject briefly to challenge our methodology in church life. In my own preaching I have noticed that the weaker my points are the more I sense a need to raise my volume. Maybe the problem is fundamentally different than what we imagine.

The first problem is foundational to our ability to live the Christian life. Perhaps the problem isn't that we have Christians sitting in our pews that are reluctant to live for Christ and who therefore need us to stir them up. Perhaps the problem is we have lost people sitting in our pews who cannot live the Christian life because the Holy Spirit does not live in them. In years of failing baptisms and loss of membership maybe we are too quick to declare someone to be "born again."

In John 4 we encounter the story of the Samaritan woman that met Jesus by Jacob's well in the heat of the day. Jesus asked her for a drink of water, and she was startled that He would cross all of the cultural barriers to initiate a conversation. He is Jewish, and she is Samaritan. His response draws her more deeply into the conversation.

"If you knew who I was, you would have asked Me for a drink of water."

She gets hung up over how Jesus can draw water without a bucket. But Jesus keeps focused.

He says, "You drink the water in this well and you will get thirsty again. But if you drink the water I give you will never be thirsty. In fact the water I give leads to eternal life."

Immediately she says, "Give me that water."

In many churches today we would have had her pray a formulaic prayer and signed her up for baptism and church membership.

The problem of sin has not been dealt with and Jesus knows it. So He is not deterred by her enthusiasm but goes back to make sure she comprehends. I have struggled with the next comment as an American, because we are so focused on the individual's responsibility that we miss cultural restrictions and even taboos.

Jesus said, "Go get your husband and bring him here." Her response lets us know that Jesus has struck the nerve of sin with this statement, but, before we go there, consider the Eastern cultural context of this instruction. In West Africa we often encounter women who will say, "I want to follow Christ, but I must ask my husband."

We don't think that way in Western contexts, but it is likely why this approach worked so well for Jesus. She admitted her sin at this point.

Once the problem of sin is laid bare, the issue becomes the confession of Christ. Jesus called attention to her marital history and she said, "I am beginning to think you must be a prophet."

So she declared her religious nature. She pointed out the difference between the Jews and Samaritans as being a matter of where you go to worship. Jesus said, it is not where you worship, but how you worship. The real difference is knowing Who you worship.

So she responded, "We know that a Messiah is coming."

Now the time is right, and Jesus says, "I am He."

When Paul preaches the gospel for the first time in Philippi the first convert is a woman from the city of Thyatira named Lydia. She doesn't have a blinding light experience like Paul's on the Damascus Road. The Scripture simply says, "The Lord opened her heart to pay attention to what was said by Paul" (Acts 16:14c). That is the mystery of salvation. The Holy Spirit has to do the work of regeneration in a person's heart. We cannot convict anyone of sin. We cannot convince them of the truth in Christ. We can only present the truth of God's Word and let the Holy Spirit take over. The reality is when a person makes a decision to become a follower of Christ, the Holy Spirit has already been working on them long before we got involved.

One night we had finished our Bible storying in the village and were going to bed. After I climbed inside the mosquito tent and lay down on the air mattress I was overwhelmed by this putrid smell.

"Sssshhhheeeeewweeee," I said. "What is that horrible smell?"

Salif, one of our translators, quickly said, "There is a dead donkey over there behind that clump of trees."

It was overwhelming and I was certain that I would never go to sleep.

"It's horrible," I said.

"Do you want me to go and burn it?" Salif asked.

"Hey, that is a great idea," I responded.

And so he got up and took kerosene and set it on fire. We all gathered around and sang "Kum-ba-yah".

Well, that is all true except for the singing. We could have taken a stick and gone over and beat the carcass and yelled, "Stop stinking, you stupid donkey."

It wouldn't have done any good because the donkey was dead. If we short circuit the work of the Holy Spirit in a person's life then we will find ourselves trying to beat the donkeys into doing what we want when they are laying on the ground dead.

The other problem may be in our discipleship methods. We gather a group together and attempt to pour an abundant amount of knowledge into their heads. We sense we have been successful because we have completed our lesson plan. We dazzled and amazed the group with our oratorical skills.

But our message never alters behavior because it doesn't penetrate the core values of the individual. God's Word is sharp and powerful. It will penetrate when we use it properly.

Two key ingredients to life-change in the area of discipleship are accountability and reproduction. Jesus would teach the crowds in parables (stories) and then He would draw aside with the disciples and explain them. Often he sent them out to make application and then had them come back and debrief.

We follow a very similar approach in West Africa and, recently, more and more I am trying to do that here. The small group that I lead ends with two basic questions:

(1.) How will you apply this to your life this week?

(2.) Whom do you know that you will share this lesson with?

Recently I was at a denominational meeting and we were having some "preacher talk" in a group of about six. One of the men looked at me and, totally changing the subject, asked, "Do you think salvation is an event, or is it a process?"

My response was, "That is a complex question that requires a conversation, not a rapidly-spewed one-word answer."

My experiences in West Africa have taught me to believe there is a process involved, but I also believe there is a point in time where a person is regenerated, or "born again."

Even when someone makes a decision to respond to the invitation of God, and prays a prayer, which I suppose is the "point in time," the Holy Spirit has been working in that person in advance, which is a process. Sometimes seeds may have been planted years ago and have been lying dormant, nourished by the prayers of intercessors, and today is the day of salvation. The conviction of sin may be a sudden realization, or a lifetime in coming. There is a real sense in my mind in which it is both. I don't remember what I said to the person that raised the question, but I saw quickly he was looking for a pigeonhole to stick me in, and I chose to drop out of the conversation. I believe there is a point where a person chooses to respond to the invitation of God to follow Jesus. The mystery of the Spirit of God is He is the One that brings about conviction of sin, confidence of truth, and conversion to Christ, in each individual. No matter how long it takes, when a person makes a decision for Christ, God the Holy Spirit takes up residence in that person. Then He reproduces the life of Christ.

The Christian life is not a life of imitation. It isn't lived by figuring out what Jesus would do and then trying to copy His behavior. If that were the case we would never live in any semblance of victory, because the Christian life is not difficult—it is impossible, in human strength. Paul said, *"I have been crucified with Christ. It is no longer I who live, but Christ Who lives in me. And the life I now live in the flesh I live by faith in the Son of God Who loved me and gave Himself for me."*(Galatians 2:20).

He is not describing a life where he imitated what Jesus did. He is describing a life where Jesus Christ lived His life through Paul. That is how it must be for each person that desires to live the real Christian life.

Consider the reminder that Jesus gave us in John 15:5. "I am the vine; you are the branches. Whoever abides in Me and I in him, he it is that bears much fruit, for apart from Me you can do nothing." He doesn't say we can do some parts of imitating Him poorly; he says we cannot do them at all. Separate the branch from the vine and it completely dies. The life of following Christ is only possible by the indwelling presence of the Holy Spirit. That is a life of God reproducing the Christ-life in us. The Bible does not describe the love, joy, peace, patience, kindness, faithfulness, gentleness, goodness, and self-control as works of the Spirit, but as fruit of the Spirit. The best works that we can produce are filthy rags.

Obviously a person who has never trusted Christ is spiritually dead. But what about the Christian that is living in disobedience to God, the carnal Christian—can we suggest that they are dead? Romans 6:16 says, *"Do you not know that if you present yourselves to anyone as obedient slaves, you are slaves of the one whom you obey, either of sin, which leads to death, or of obedience, which leads to righteousness?"* When a person lives in disobedience to God, sin reigns, and sin always leads to death. A carnal Christian may very well die and go to heaven, but that does not mean they are experiencing spiritual life while they are physically alive and in broken fellowship with God. They have grieved the Holy Spirit and therefore a sense of death reigns in their life. So if we are not careful, we may find ourselves beating dead donkeys with sticks. What is needed—whether a person is unregenerate and lost, or they are backslidden and therefore carnal—is the *"breath of the living God"* in their lives.

Certainly God uses the living Word to quicken hearts. The power of the Word, however, is not in the delivery. It is the breath of God. It is the Holy Spirit quickening someone's heart to hear and receive.

"We Have Never Heard That Name Before"

Chapter 11

"How then will they call on Him in Whom they have not believed? And how are they to believe in Him of Whom they have never heard?" (Romans 10:14)

"We have never heard that name, Isa (Jesus), before," the Imam and the chief said to me. They had come along with the elders of their village to pick up the food we were distributing. But I am getting ahead of myself and need to tell you what was happening from the beginning.

Many of our trips have a similar nature to them. For the first three years we literally sent a team every six to eight weeks focused on discipling the believers in F-village, and modeling evangelism every opportunity we had.

In May 2008, our missionary partner, Steve, called me and said, "The believers in your village and in the surrounding areas are eating grass. They are out of food and the harvest is not until November."

"What are we going to do?" I asked.

"That is why I am calling," Steve responded. "Baptist Global Relief is going to give us some money to distribute Millet. We are going to feed about 32,000 people in 61 different villages."

"Who is we," I laughed, "Are you French, or is there a mouse in your pocket?"

"Very funny," Steve continued, "I am calling to see if you can organize a group to come and distribute the food."

"How many people do we need?" I asked. "How are we going to feed that many people? How quick do you need us to come? I don't know if I can pull that off or not. Wow, are you serious?"

I had hundreds of questions racing through my mind, but for the moment I immediately dispatched a prayer request through our email prayer-line.

Over the next two weeks a team of ten came together. Three other churches in our association supplied some participants. We immediately began orientation with the folks planning to go and coordination with the missionaries in Mali.

"We will work off the last government registration," Steve suggested. "We will distribute food based on the number of people in each household and by villages. We will work in two distribution points, so you will need to divide your team into two groups."

The basic food item in the bush where we work is millet. To me it looks a lot like the birdseed I put in my bird feeder at home. It is more durable in the rugged climate than other crops, and more nutritious than many. We were going to distribute over 500 tons of millet in approximately 5 days work time. Each village would send representatives to our distribution points and pick up the food for their village. The food would be given to nonbelievers, Muslims, and Christians alike. We split the team into two groups of five to work from two different distribution points, one of which was F-village.

There was quite a buzz of excitement when we arrived in the village.

"Ini se," I said as I got off the bus to the group of believers that were gathered at our hut. That is a basic salutation to a group. In the south we would say, "Hi, ya'll."

The village men responded, "M'ba. N'se," an acknowledgement of my greeting, and a greeting in return.

"Aw kakene?" (Are you well?), I asked.

"Toro te", (Pronounced "torahtay" and it loosely translates, no problem, but in this context would mean, we are well.)

We proceeded through the litany of greetings that are appropriate. In this culture, greetings are very important, and relationships are everything. We ask all of the participants to learn and practice the greetings, although we rely on translators for the rest of our communication.

It is a lesson in patience to go through a translator to communicate with someone else, as well as to go through the extended greeting ritual. But, because of the value of relationships, time is of little consequence.

There were a number of people there to greet us in addition to the believers from the church. Some of the elders and a representative from the mayor's office were also present. After the greetings, the next statement was, "Can you pray for rain?"

"Abba, Father, in the name of Jesus Who is the Christ, we pray that you might send rain, Amen."

The rest of that day was spent setting up our base camp at the hut, and preparing for the food distribution to begin in the morning. About 10:30 that evening we set up our mosquito tents to sleep outside. The stars were out, and the moon was bright. In the far distant northeast we could see some lightning but thought it might miss us. How is that for practicing faith in the prayers we offered?

As I lay down to sleep it became obvious that the storm was moving our way.

"Father," I prayed. "I really don't want to sleep inside that mud hut. It gets so hot in there, and it is so nice out here tonight. Could you hold the rain until tomorrow?"

Immediately I was overwhelmed with a sense of shame at having uttered such a selfish prayer. It was as if God said to my heart, "These people are starving and they need rain for the harvest for next year, and all you care about is the comfort of this one night's sleep."

"Father, please forgive me for being so selfish. Of course I would rather you send rain than for me to be comfortable."

As an act of faith, I got up and started carrying my stuff inside to get set up for the evening.

Buddy was in another tent next to me and he said, "You really think it is going to rain?"

He along with Beth and Embree were on their first trip to the village and had come to help with the food distribution. Angela was also with us, but she had been before.

"I am pretty sure it is going to rain and pretty soon."

Buddy got up and began carrying his stuff in with me.

Embree said, "I am staying outside as long as possible. I think it might pass us by."

Buddy and I set up inside the men's side of the hut, and left a spot for Embree to join us.

It was only about 20 minutes before the rain hit and Embree was scurrying inside. Even with the door shut, water runs inside. Buddy and I bit our lips to keep from laughing as Embree lined the crack under the door with layer after layer of toilet paper until it was like some kind of paper mache' door-stop.

The storm came and went, and we opened the windows and the door, but stayed inside for the night.

The next morning was a beautiful day and we got up, prepared breakfast and got ready to distribute the food. Some folks came by our hut from a village several kilometers away.

Their greeting was abrupt, "We want to meet the rainmaker."

They wanted to meet me, the one that had prayed for rain, but what an incredible witness opportunity.

I was able to say, "I know the Rainmaker and I would be glad to introduce you."

Because the majority of folks in these villages have little awareness of the Biblical worldview, it is necessary to give a general outline. . So, our basic gospel presentation often begins with the story of creation and a summary of Old Testament developments moving to the story of Christ and the cross as a culmination.

On that first day, Steve arrived about mid-day to see how things were going. He had spent the night in the other distribution village, J-village. We had a different team of 5, Mason, Furman, Bob, Johnny, and Paul working there. When Steve arrived, he looked at me and said, "The rainmaker, huh?"

"Where did you hear that," I asked.

"Word travels fast in the bush, "he answered with a big smile.

On another trip, our team was asked to pray for rain. I wasn't on this trip, but our team prayed for these men, and for rain.

It rained almost immediately. The four men who had requested prayer shared with our team members that they had first gone to the Imam and asked him to pray.

The Imam had said, "I can pray for rain, but it may take a couple of years for God to answer. The Christians are in town, why don't you go ask them. God always answers their prayers."

What an incredible statement! That Imam recognized the power of Jesus' name!

In West Africa, contracts in the bush are verbal. The larger the group that witnesses the agreement, the stronger and more binding is the contract. Therefore, we required that each village send a delegation to come and pick up their food and we made them wait until the whole group was there. Prior to giving them the bags of millet, I shared a very subtle and brief presentation of the gospel.

"Christian believers in America heard that you were hungry, they were moved with compassion and they took up money and bought food to share with you. They did this because God took compassion on us and provided a way that we might know Him. He came into the world in the person of Jesus Christ. This Jesus loves you and He will help you if you trust in Him. There are some Christians here in F-village and if you want to know more about what I am saying, talk with them."

Then I would introduce a couple of the believers from the village and have prayer with the group before they received their food.

The West Africans want to be good hosts and they will do what they can to please us when we are there. Additionally, most of them would automatically think that in order to receive the food they were required to pray the prayer. Therefore we did not call for a response, we elected to let the Holy Spirit prompt hearts and lead people to come and inquire for more information.

Several of the leaders from a variety of villages said the same thing to me. They came and thanked us for the food.

"In another month we would likely begin to die without this help."

Again and again, they would say, "We have never heard this name, 'Jesus,' before."

It suddenly became clear. So many people in our world have not rejected the gospel, saying "No" to Jesus, they simply have never heard the message.

The Scripture came into focus: "For everyone who calls on the name of the Lord will be saved. How then will they call on Him in Whom they have not believed? And how are they to believe in Him of Whom they have never heard? And how are they to hear without someone preaching? And how are they to preach unless they are sent? As it is written, "How beautiful are the feet of those who preach the good news!" (Romans 10:13-15, ESV)

There are approximately 12,000 different people groups that have been identified in our world, and approximately 3800 of those people groups (1.7 billion people) have no access to the gospel message. That is a staggering reality that we should all find unacceptable.

As western Christians, we have a hard time comprehending that there is anyone left in our day and time who does not have access to the message of Christ. The reality, however, that at least 1.7 billion people have never heard is a statistic we must not ignore.

But there are indeed multitudes of people in this world where there is no Gospel witness and no strategy

Our people group numbers over 4 million. They are considered an unreached people group because so few are believers. Mission agencies define a people group as unreached when less than 2% of them are Christian. Our people group has less than .001% that are believers.

What does a group of four million people even look like? That day we provided food for 32,000 people from 61 villages. That is an image I can comprehend. That is less than half the number of people that attend a major college football event on any given Saturday in America, which is why I know what 80,000 people in one-place looks like. Take that number and cut in half and scatter them in 61 different clusters over a region with a radius of about 35 to 40 miles.

Most of these people had never heard the name of Jesus, much less the gospel message. Who will tell them?

On this particular trip it became clear to me that I cannot reach 32,000 people, or 4 million, much less 1.7 billion. I could go to a different village everyday on each trip and share the gospel with a place it has never been before. If I did that on every trip I could not get to all the villages to which we distributed food, much less get to 4 million people.

That is why our objective is to help equip a church of indigenous people who will assume responsibility for making and teaching disciples in their people group.

That afternoon I gathered three of the leaders of the church and cast vision for evangelizing the villages around us. "I can never get to all of the villages on my own. God wants you to take responsibility for your people." We studied the Great Commission again.

"Which villages will you each be responsible for?" I asked. Each of the three men named a couple of villages they would take responsibility for going weekly to preach the Word of God.

"What day of the week will you go each week, and who will you take with you to assist?" They assured me of their days and who would go with them. Together we prayed for the spread of the gospel throughout all of West Africa, and especially among this people group.

Retrospect

Shortly after our first trip to West Africa, I was attending a meeting of an association of churches in our city. The director of missions had asked me to share a brief testimony of what God was doing, and then he told the association they were going to partner with us. A conversation had followed explaining that there were many people groups in our world with no access at all to the Gospel.

An elderly man from one of the churches raised his hand, and then asked, "Are you telling me that after all the years we have supported mission work around the world, and after all the money we have given to international missions, there are still people who have never heard the message?"

At first, I wasn't sure whether to laugh or cry. Can anyone be that ignorant of the facts? Indeed, there are many in our churches that do not know the facts.

There are places where people still say, "I have never heard that name before."

Some of our translators in West Africa become extremely good friends. None have been any closer to me that Isaac. One Sunday afternoon in our village it was a particularly hot day. Our ice had run out a couple of days earlier and we were drinking lukewarm to hot water. I don't remember how the subject came up, but I jokingly said to Isaac, "I will love you forever if you bring me a cold Coke." Shortly Isaac said, "Here, Brad. Here is your coke." I was resting in a hammock under the hangar in front of our house, and I was opening my eyes carefully anticipating some prank to be pulled. Shock is the best description of my reaction, however, when I realized Isaac had a coke for me, and it was reasonably cold.

"Where did you find that?" I asked. "Down in the village," he said. "There is a drink machine powered by a generator."

"Wow," I thought. "This is uptown."

Think about the implications of this. Coca-cola can get its message to a remote village of West Africa, and yet it was 2007 before the Gospel of Jesus Christ ever made it. How messed up is that?

My 15-year-old daughter recently went on a mission trip to New York City. In a phone call home she said to her mom, "It is going to be so hard to leave these people to come home. Mom, I had a child ask me, 'What's a Bible?' and then she told me she had never heard of Jesus before."

From the cities of the United States to the bush country of West Africa, there are still billions of people who have not heard the good news of Jesus Christ in a clear compelling way. *Whoever calls on the name of the Lord will be saved. But how can they call on Him of whom they have never heard?"*

Can a Log Become a Crocodile?
Chapter 12

"Therefore, if anyone is in Christ he is a new creation."
(2 Cor. 5:17)

The people group we work with in West Africa love to quote African proverbs. Sometimes they don't translate well into English, but in some cases they make perfect sense. On one of our trips I armed myself with some proverbs to use with Bible stories, thinking that it might grip their hearts more effectively if I used a bridge they were familiar with. One such proverb says, "No matter how long a log floats in the river, it will never become a crocodile."

During our teaching time, I said, "I want to quote an African proverb." Immediately big smiles broke out on everyone's face. I said, "I have been told that there is an African proverb that says, 'No matter how long a log floats in the river, it will never become a crocodile.'" Then I continued, "Are you familiar with this proverb." "O wo" (Yes) they said, as they all nodded in agreement.

"What does it mean?" I asked.

"It means that you cannot be something that you are not," was the loose translation of the answer they gave.

"So what if I take the log out of the river and carve it to look like a crocodile, and put it back in the river and leave it for a long time—will it become a crocodile?" I asked.

119

"Ayi" (No, and it is pronounced eye-ee), they replied in chorus.

"What if I take it to the witch doctor and he does his magic, will it turn into a crocodile?" I asked them.

"Ayi."

"Is there anything that can change this log into a crocodile?" I asked one more time.

"Ayi."

I was holding a stick, much like the staff of a shepherd. So I asked, *"What about this stick? Can it turn into a snake?"*

"Ayi," they emphatically declared.

"What if I throw it down into the dirt? Will it become a snake?"

"Ayi, ayi, ayi."

"Are you sure?" I asked, although I was tempted to say, 'Is that your final answer."

"We are sure," they declared.

"I want to tell you a story," I said. "This is a story that comes from the Word of God. This is not a story made up by men, but a true story from God's Word. This story is about one of God's Old Testament prophets by the name of Moses. Do you remember the story of Moses we told before?"

"O-wo" (Yes), the Africans answered.

"In case some of you have forgotten, Moses was a man born while God's people were living as slaves in a country called Egypt. Remember when he was born, the king of Egypt had issued a law that the first born of all the people of Israel be put to death. Moses' mother had placed him in a basket made of reeds and lined with pitch and set him out on the river. The king of Egypt's daughter had found the baby Moses and had taken him in and raised him as her own.

"Well, as a young man Moses stepped into an argument between an Egyptian and a Hebrew, and he had killed the Egyptian. Because he was afraid, Moses had fled to the back-side of the desert. There he had married, and the story I want to tell you is about Moses one day when he was shepherding his father-in-law's sheep."

"One day as Moses was taking care of the sheep, he saw a strange sight on the side of the mountain. There was a bush burning, but it was not being consumed. So Moses went up to this strange sight. As Moses approached the bush, he heard a voice speak.

'Moses, Moses!'

And Moses said, 'Here I am.'

Then the voice said, 'Do not come near; first take the sandals off of your feet because you are standing on holy ground. I am the God of your father, the God of Abraham, the God of Isaac, and the God of Jacob.'

Moses hid his face, because he was afraid to look at God.

Then the Lord said to Moses, 'I have seen all of the suffering of my people living in Egypt, and I have heard their cries to me, and I have come to deliver them out of the hands of the Egyptians and take them to a land that is good, and a land flowing with milk and honey.'

Then the Lord said to Moses, 'I will send you to deliver my people from the king of Egypt and from their slavery.'

But Moses said to God, 'Who am I that the king of Egypt will listen to me?'

Then God said to Moses, 'I will be with you.'

And Moses said, 'If I tell the people of Israel that God has sent me to deliver them, they will ask me, 'What is His name?' What do I tell them. God said, 'I am who I am. Tell them 'I am' has sent you.'

Moses said, 'They will not believe me.'

So God said to Moses, 'What is that in your hand?'

And Moses answered God and said, 'It is a staff.'

So God said, 'Throw it down.'

And Moses threw the staff to the ground, and it turned into a snake."

At this point, I threw the stick in my hand dramatically to the ground in front of me. Those who were sitting right in front all jumped, which caused everyone to laugh.

Then I smiled, and said, 'What would you have done if that stick I was holding turned into a snake?"

One of the men said, "I would have run," and the others affirmed that is what they would have done also.

I said, 'Me too," and we all laughed.

"Well, Moses threw the stick down and it turned into a snake and the Word of God says, 'Moses ran from it.' But the Lord said to Moses, 'Put out your hand and pick it back up.'

And so Moses reached down and caught the snake by the tail and it turned into a staff again.

God gave Moses a couple other signs he could show the people and told him to go and do as he had been told. And

Moses told his father-in-law and headed back to obey God. This is a story from the Word of God."

We always book end the Bible stories with this statement so that the group listening can distinguish between what is the Bible story and what are our own comments. That is just one of the guidelines to remember in a setting where people do not read. It is also important to avoid using pronouns, such as "He told him to go and do this." Even though it may seem redundant to us, we want to avoid confusion about who told whom, so we always supply the names: "God told Moses." We also try to limit the number of names in the story to three or less so that the hearers can remember. Most importantly, while it is alright to leave out some of the details, it is never alright to ad-lib anything that is not in the Bible. Some preachers have a bad habit of sermonizing and adding opinions or interpretations. Tell the story as God's Word tells it.

One of the goals when we tell a story is to tell the story up to five or more times, so that the listeners can remember the story and be able to tell it themselves.

Having told the story, I revisited my original questions. I said, "Can this stick in my hand ever become a snake?"

"A-ye (No)," was the unanimous response."

"Are you sure?" I asked.

"Yes, we are sure," they replied.

"What happened in the story with the stick in Moses hand?" I questioned.

"It turned into a snake," they responded.

"So sometimes sticks can become snakes," I commented.

"O-wo (Yes)," they said.

"When can a stick become a snake?" I asked.

"When God changes it into a snake?" They asked in response.

"Ah-ha," I said with as much enthusiasm as I could express, and they all laughed. "So God can change a stick into a snake?"

"O-wo (Yes)," came the reply.

"Let me ask you another question. Remember the proverb we started with?"

"O-wo," they said.

"So can a log floating in the river ever become a crocodile?" I asked.

"A-yee (No)," they declared enthusiastically.

"Never?" I asked.

"Never," they replied.

"So," I began. "Is it harder for a log to become a crocodile than it is for a stick to become a snake?"

They gave me a puzzled look.

"Let me ask it differently. What happened to the stick in our story?"

"It became a snake," they declared.

"Why did it become a snake?" I asked.

"Because God changed it," they said.

"OK, then, let me see if I understand. God can change sticks into snakes, but he cannot change logs into crocodiles," I said with a look of some seriousness on my face.

The Africans began to smile and they said, "We understand. A log can become a crocodile when God changes it."

"Do you remember what you told me the proverb about the log becoming a crocodile means?" I asked.

"O-wo (Yes)," they replied. "It means you cannot be something that you are not."

"The reason that I am telling you this story and asking these questions is more important than whether or not God can change a stick into a snake. We know God can do anything," I said. "The real question that I want you to think about is, 'Can God change a man from being a sinner into being righteous so that the man can have a personal relationship to a Holy God?"

"Sin-ay, can you help me," I asked as I motioned for him to step up beside me. I turned him sideway, and I turned sideways and stood right behind him. "Look at us," I said. "I want you to notice how we are different." As I pointed to his stomach, I exaggerated mine even more by poking it out as far as I could, and I said, "Can you see anything different about us?"

"O-wo (Yes)," they said. "You are billy-billy-bah." (That loosely translates, 'You are big and fat.'). I reminded them that some of them had once told me I was indeed bigger than a donkey.

"So what about Sin-ay?" I asked.

"He is fit-ten-nay, fit-ten-nay." (Which I am told means he has a skinny butt. Probably a comment that will earn you some brownie points if you use it on your wife, guys.)

"Can he ever be billy-billy-ba?" I asked.

"If you feed him," they laughed.

"Is there anything else different about us?" I asked.

"O-wo (Yes)," they said. "He is an African and you are an American."

"So can an American ever become an African, or an African become an American?" I asked.

"Ah-ee (No)," they quickly said.

"Wait a minute," I responded." In America, someone can become an American citizen and get papers from the government."

They nodded their heads affirmatively, and said, "Oh, yes, you can do that here too."

"Is there anything else different about Sin-ay and me?" I asked. "He is black, and you are white," one of them said.

"Can a white man ever become black?" I asked.

"A-ee (No)," they all said.

"Or, can a black man ever become white?" I asked.

"A-ee (No),' they quickly responded.

"Can a stick become a snake?" I asked one more time.

"Only if God changes it," they said.

"Can a log ever become a crocodile? I asked again.

"Only if God changes it," they said once more in unison.

"Then let me ask you this again? Can a white man ever become black?" I asked.

"Only if God changes him," one of them said, and then all agreed.

"OK, here is the point. In order to have a personal relationship with God, we have to have hearts of righteousness. We have already discovered that we have hearts that are full of sin and disobedience. So here is the most important question of all today. How can sinful man become righteous in the eyes of God? How can our sinful hearts be made clean so we can have a relationship to God?" I asked.

"Only God can do that," one of them said, and the others agreed.

"That is right," I affirmed. "Listen to what God says in His Word. "Therefore, if anyone is in Christ, he is a new creation. The old has passed away; behold, the new has come'.""

"So how does God change a man from being a sinner into a righteous man? I asked.

"Let me tell you the Word of God on this one more time. 'Therefore, if anyone is in Christ, he is a new creation. The old has passed away; behold, the new has come.' How does a man become righteous according to that scripture?"

"Only by becoming a believer in Christ," one of them answered.

"That is right," I said. "Only in Christ."

"Because this is a new story," I said, "and because it is getting late, we won't continue tonight. I will teach you this story in the morning so that you can tell it to others. But before we pray, what do you think that the main lesson in this entire story is?"

A discussion took place for about ten minutes between the Africans. Then finally, one became the spokesman through the translator. "The only way a sinful person can be righteous in God's eyes is by coming to Jesus."

"That is right. That is very good." I said, and called on one of them to pray.

After the prayer, through the translator they asked for the road. It is polite to seek permission to leave in this culture, and that is the way it is done. You ask for the road of your host. So I agreed, and we all began to shake hands, saying to one another, "Kum-bay," which essentially means, "I will see you later."

Normally we would ask more questions about application, and we would repeat the story for them to learn it. Then they would practice it with each other. Using a translator, this story is longer than most, and it was late. We would begin again here the next morning.

Retrospect

We learned first-hand working in Mali how powerful stories are. We have become so caught up in the special effects of the movie industry that we might overlook this fact. In the village of West Africa that the church I pastored spent more than 5 years working in, TV's are very rare. When they have them they are powered by batteries like we have in our car, and they have very limited choice, usually one channel carrying news or a soccer game. When you tell a story, you create an image that plays in their mind and it has tremendous impact.

Personally, I think storying is usually more effective than an outline well thought-out and delivered.

I have sought through this little book to tell stories from my experiences in both Africa and America. I pray that someone identifies with these stories and finds direction and hope along the journey through this life. More significantly, I pray that it somehow stirs up in your heart a desire to impact the lostness of the nations of the world, especially those who have no access to the gospel. These stories carry us to about the halfway point of my Malian journey. It is a good stopping place, and if the Lord wills, I can finish the journey in a sequel. So to that end, I offer these "tales of a donkey" **until all have heard.**

The Donkey Method
(Like the Camel Method, but Different)
Epilogue

"They brought the donkey and the colt and put on them their cloaks, and He sat on them." (Matthew 21:7)

The word for donkey appears in the Bible approximately 154 times. They are beasts of burden. Quite often in the Bible we see them as a means of transportation or other menial labor. There is probably no more significant occasion of a donkey being put into the service of God than the triumphal entry into Jerusalem by the Lord on Palm Sunday. So significant is this event that all four Gospels record it. Mark and Luke simply tell us it was a colt, but Matthew and John refer to it as a donkey. We are also told in Matthew and John that it is a fulfillment of Zechariah 9:9. "Rejoice greatly, O daughter of Zion!. Shout aloud, O daughter of Jerusalem! Behold, your king is coming to you; righteous and having salvation is he, humble and mounted on a donkey, on a colt, the foal of a donkey."

The camel method is a methodology of presenting the gospel in Muslim countries. It is described in a book entitled, *The Camel.*[10] This method derives its name from a Muslim Proverb that says, "And we know that Allah has one hundred names. And that he has revealed 99 of his names to the sons of men that they may know and worship him. But one name, the one-hundredth name, he has told only to the camel. And, the

---

[10] Kevin Greeson, 2007; *The Camel.* Wigtake Resources.

131

camel, he is not talking."Like so many other things in Christian history, the camel method has raised some controversy and debate among some Christian groups.

It started as a joke between a friend and me after I wrote the first couple of chapters. By email I sent the first chapters to him with a title page, "The donkey method". He sent it back with a picture of a donkey and a subtitle, "Like the Camel Method, but different." The idea began to take life in my head. As far as I know, no one else has proposed the "donkey method."The Scriptures describing Jesus' triumphal entry into Jerusalem on the back of a donkey outline the points for us.

1. God, is the only rightful recipient of our worship.

2. God, the King has come to establish His kingdom.

3. The world does not know or honor Him.

4. God is willing to use anyone who is willing to be surrendered fully to Him, to carry the gospel of the Kingdom to the people groups of the earth.

Jesus said, "And this gospel of the kingdom will be proclaimed throughout the whole world as a testimony to all nations, and then the end will come" (Matthew 24:14). We know that we are responsible as followers of Jesus Christ to present His gospel to the world. His gospel is a kingdom gospel. One of the essentials of a kingdom is a king. The gospel message tells us that our King has come. He came as a baby born in Bethlehem and was placed in a cow's eating trough. He grew up and then began a ministry of teaching God's way while He was walking among men. Most significantly, He never sinned, and He willingly gave His life on a cross as a substitute for us. This King was killed, buried, and then rose from the dead. He remained with His disciples and friends for 40 days and returned to the Father, but with the great promise that He would come again and establish His kingdom rule on earth.

The "donkey method" is simply carrying the Gospel of the Kingdom to all the nations of the world, which means all of the people groups of the world. It recognizes that a donkey is one that exists for the pleasure and service of its master, its owner. The donkey method involves a person like you or me recognizing that as a Christian we have been bought and paid for by the King. Knowing that we belong to Him we also understand it is our responsibility to carry our King to all people so that He will be given the honor and glory that He is due.

Donkeys ultimately don't have any choice about what they are put in service to do. I have watched small children in Africa put donkeys to work. They need prodding and encouraging from time to time. But by and large the donkey has little say in the matter. We start out with a lot of "say-so" about our lives. The Bible tells us, however, to present ourselves to God completely. Someone has suggested that the answer is "Yes" to God, and then we say, "Oh, what was the question?" If we put our "Yes" on God's altar in surrender, doesn't He have the right to determine where on the map we serve Him? Shouldn't we be seeking to go wherever He desires and to do whatever He wants?

The donkey method simply suggests that we are to be surrendered servants to the King. It is our responsibility to take King Jesus wherever He wants to go. We know from His instructions that He wants to go where they have never heard His name before. The apostle Paul certainly understood that.

.He said, *". . . thus I make it my ambition to preach the gospel, not where Christ has already been named, lest I build on someone else's foundation"* (Romans 15:20).

When Beulah Baptist church began its journey into international mission involvement, not a single one of us had any idea what we were becoming involved in. We might have shied away had we actually known everything. We entered into a journey that said, "Yes, Lord, we will follow You and go where You take us."

Everyone can do this. Any church can do this.

Consider the difference in us saying "We can't" and saying, "We won't." Paul wrote to the believers in Phillipi, *"I can do all things through Christ Who strengthens me"* (Phil. 4:13). Are we willing to say that something is too difficult for God to accomplish through us? Let's put aside our excuses and start asking God where and when?

When I was involved in Campus Crusade for Christ while in college, one young lady that I challenged to be in a discipleship group said to me, "Brad, did you ever think that discipleship is not for everybody."

After reflecting on that, I said, "In my opinion discipleship is for everyone, but not everyone is for discipleship." Maybe that applies to this setting as well. I think the problem isn't that *missions isn't intended for everyone, but that not everyone is willing to engage in missions*.

Would you consider saying, "God, where do you want me to go?" Instead of trying to figure it all out, why not trust the King to show you where He wants you to go and how to get there. Maybe your prayer should be, "Father, I am planning to go, but I am willing to stay."

A friend of mine once said to me, "Either go or cash flow." He went on to say, "Because I have no intention of going, I will help support others to go."

I don't think I can completely agree with him, but I at least appreciate the fact that he recognizes that every Christian has some responsibility in this matter of missions. All of us can pray. Every Christian can and should pray for the work of missions around the world. We can pray for unreached and unengaged mission groups by name. We can pray that God will send laborers into the harvest, especially to these unreached, unengaged people groups. We can pray for specific workers around the world that we know.

Most Christians can support the work of missions internationally with their finances. I believe that all Christians can do this, but I will allow for the exception that some may not be able to do much. The wisdom of God's tithe suggests that everyone can do something, based on each person's ability.

It has been said that about 80% of the resources of the world is in the hands of about 20% of the people. Most Americans that I know would exclude themselves from the ranks of the wealthy, but that is only a matter of perspective. Compared to most of the world we are all in that 20% category. We no doubt spend way too much money on our pleasures. One trip to a majority-world country can change the perspective of most—maybe all—Christians. We can all support the work of missions with our pocketbooks, and we can do it to a greater degree than we are currently doing.

Finally, many Christians can actually go on some type of short-term missions endeavor. God may not have called you to be a career missionary. But we are all included in the Great Commission, and if we can go, I think we should go. If not for the benefit of those who have never heard, we should go in order to allow God to change our lives in relationship to His Great Commission task. It will open our eyes to the way the 80% live and hopefully open our hearts to do all we can, to be sure that all will hear.

As I write this, I am aware that there are 46,000 churches in our Southern Baptist denomination, and only approximately 120 of those churches have accepted responsibility for a people group hearing the gospel. There are not enough missionaries and there is not enough money to leave this responsibility to mission boards and agencies alone. Together we can ensure that no one has to ever say again, "I have never heard this name before."

My prayer is that you have read this book with a growing awareness that if God can use an old donkey like me, He can also use you. If God can take a small blue-collar church in a rural community of South Carolina on 26 mission trips in less than six years, He can use the church where you are. God can do it through each of us working together until all have heard.

I have not attempted to draw out every lesson in these stories. I have attempted to tell the stories as accurately as my memory serves. I have discovered in the bush country of Mali that if I tell the Bible stories, the people listening become my teachers. You may see lessons I have missed. I hope you enjoyed the stories. More importantly, I hope you will see the potential for God to use you.

Until all have heard.